MW00613057

SINGING
THE SONG
of
SONGS

SINGING THE SONG *of* SONGS

HOW TO LOVE YOUR SPOUSE LIKE JESUS LOVES HIS

GREG BIRDWELL

1THING PUBLISHING
CINCINNATI, OHIO

Copyright © 2020 by Greg Birdwell

All rights reserved. No part of this book may be reproduced, stored in a retrieval system, or transmitted in any form or by any means—electronic, mechanical, photocopy, recording, or otherwise—except for brief quotations for the purpose of review or comment, without the prior written permission of the publisher, 1 Thing Publishing.

Requests for information should be addressed to:
1 Thing Publishing, *8120 Glenridge Court, West Chester, Ohio 45069*

ISBN: 978-0-578-65704-2

Unless otherwise noted, scripture quotations are from the ESV® Bible (The Holy Bible, English Standard Version®), copyright 2001 by Crossway, a publishing ministry of Good News Publishers. Used by permission. All rights reserved.

Scripture quotations marked (NASB) are taken from the NEW AMERICAN STANDARD BIBLE®, Copyright © 1960, 1962, 1963, 1968, 1971, 1972, 1973, 1975, 1977, 1995 by The Lockman Foundation. Used by permission.

Italicized text within a biblical quotation represents the author's emphasis.

Cover design: germancreative

For Shelby
Most beautiful among women
My lily among brambles

CONTENTS

Acknowledgements

Thank you to those who initially encouraged me to do this, including a few of my fellow elders at Providence Bible Fellowship: Rick Jones, Jason Odel, and John Botkin. Thanks to others at Providence who have prayed and offered encouragement.

Thank you to the editorial team. First, my project manager and first reader, Greg Tickle. Brother, only you, I, and the Lord know how much you improved this book. Everyone else saw it after you made such insightful recommendations for changes. Additionally, your management of the whole process saved me so much time and allowed me to just write. I truly feel like we did this book together. I can't thank you enough.

Glenn Larue, what a blessing it was for the Lord to cause our paths to cross. I've been encouraged just to spend time with you, but your comments and recommendations were incredibly helpful. If I can ever return the favor, I'd be happy to do so.

Susan Carter, you dear saint! Thanks for praying, encouraging, editing/proofreading, and giving some much-needed (did I use that hyphen correctly?) counsel about how to manage this endeavor. Of all the souls with which I've had the pleasure to worship, yours is among the most delightfully Christ-exalting. Miss you dearly.

Rylie Harrison, I'm so grateful you offered to take one last look at this. My soul, that's a fine-toothed comb you have! What a blessing to have a professional in the family.

Thanks to those in my family who took the time to read so much of this thing as I wrote it. Dad, Christi…and Mom. I love you, Mom. You read every word of this and were faithful to call me and give me your thoughts. The Lord always sent those phone calls when my enthusiasm was beginning to flag. I still love talking about eternal things with you.

Thanks to my kids for not being impressed with me. I love being "just Dad" to y'all.

Finally, thank you to my wife, Shelby, for supporting me in everything I do. You are a delight, and I adore you. I'm grateful to be singing the Song with *you*.

01

CORRECTING THE MUSIC

"Is this all there is?"

After thirteen years, three children, and virtually no improvement in her marriage, Vanessa's question was an honest one. Her husband Dan worked hard and came home spent, while Vanessa did laundry, cleaned, and worked part-time to make ends meet. They navigated a blur of kids' sports and music lessons, sleeping in the same bed every night, yet not knowing each other any better than they did five years ago.

Vanessa did not know that Dan had the same question. "Is this all there is? Are we marking time only to die? Are the kids our only, our best contribution to the world?"

Over the years, they'd seen Christian counselors, attended marriage conferences, and listened to hours of "relevant, practical" sermons. All the counsel they'd received and tried could fit into one of three buckets: "spice it up," "pray more, try harder," and "give, in order to get." At the end of each attempt, their frustrations were more ingrained, emotions more seared, hearts more distant.

So they did what countless other Christian couples do: they lowered their expectations to reflect their reality. Slowly the question, "Is this all there is?" became less of a question and more of a signpost marking the end of a more hopeful time.

Sadly, Dan and Vanessa do not represent the outliers of modern Christian marriage. If you are married and have spent much time at all on this side of the honeymoon, you may have thought and felt the same things. There was a time of great hope before the wedding. There were those rough days of early marriage when the shiny veneer wore off and you realized your spouse wasn't perfect after all. However, you still had the rest of your life to reform them, and you refused to give up. But one day, after years of tears and effort, pain and forgiveness, perhaps you found yourself asking something like, "Is this all there is?"

But is disappointment or disillusionment inevitable? Most of us can hardly give in to the idea that it is. Like Dan and Vanessa, many of us exhaust ourselves trying to change our spouses or ourselves. Or we give up on one marriage, cast it away, and look for another. For others, a biblical commitment to never divorce leads them to settle for the unfulfilling marriage they ended up with. Even at that, no one wants to believe it was inevitable. We may convince ourselves, "I just married the wrong person. It could have been different with someone else." The last thing we want is to admit that this is indeed all there is.

Our Trajectory

The aim of this chapter is to answer two questions:

- What are the foundational problems that lead to difficulty and disillusionment in marriage?
- Where do we find the solution to these problems?

In a nutshell, we have two foundational problems. First, we tend to look to marriage, rather than Christ, as our ultimate fulfillment. Second, we conceive of marriage as a vehicle for self-fulfillment rather than loving self-sacrifice. We have been trying to sing a song, as it were, reading the wrong music in the wrong key. The solution is found in the Scriptures in a better song, the Song of Songs, better known as the Song of Solomon, where both foundational errors are corrected.

The Wrong Music

When I was in high school, I played percussion in the school band. I'm not sure what it is about Texas band directors, but in my experience, most of them could have had distinguished careers as mafia enforcers or CIA hitmen. What leads so many of them to teach the arts in the Lone Star State is a mystery to me. Anyway, for a week straight I drew the unwanted and loud vocal attention of the band director due to my inability to correctly play one particular piece of music. I was a decent player and knew how to count, but no matter how much he berated me in front of the whole band, I could not play the right rhythm at the right time. Every day it was the same thing, so that toward the end of the week, when he said we were going to rehearse that piece, the whole room looked at me with a mixture of sympathy and horror.

"Bring your music over here!" the director yelled. "It can't be that hard to read!" As he compared my music to his score, the proverbial lightbulb came on above his head. I had been playing music wrongly titled; though the title looked the same, I was playing a completely different piece of music than the rest of the band.

Correcting the music in marriage in most cases isn't a matter of merely getting on the same tempo with our spouse. Many of us are reading the wrong music. Yet, it's not that the husband and wife aren't reading the same music, but both husband and wife aren't reading the same music as God! Instead of a symphony, the only thing that can result is a cacophony.

The material difference between the music God has written and what we typically try to play is this: God's music holds up Himself as the ultimate fulfillment of the human heart, while too many Christian husbands and wives are reading music of the world's making, which holds that marriage itself is the ultimate fulfillment of the human heart. At the end of the day, this is a worship problem. Our search for ultimate fulfillment in something other than God constitutes idolatry and is doomed to end in misery.

It may seem strange to think of fulfillment in marriage as an idol, but an idol is anything that consistently eclipses God in our attention, desire, devotion, and choices.[1] Idols can be inherently sinful things like pornography and drunkenness, but they don't have to be. In fact, it is far more likely that the typical Christian will idolize things that are not

---

[1] Stuart Scott, *The Exemplary Husband: A Biblical Perspective* (Bemidji, MN: Focus Pub., 2002), 91.

inherently evil--gifts given to us by God. It's a common tool of the enemy to tempt us to value the gift over the Giver.

This is a point of the passage in Romans 1:18-32, which catalogs the fallen human propensity to trade worship of the Creator for worship of created things. "Claiming to be wise, they became fools, and exchanged the glory of the immortal God for images resembling mortal man and birds and animals and creeping things...and worshiped and served the creature rather than the Creator..." (Rom. 1:22-23, 25b). The result of idolatry is that man is given over to his sinful passions and self-deception.

God intends for our highest fulfillment to come from our relationship with Him. Just listen to these thoughts from Psalm 16:

> I say to the LORD, 'You are my Lord; I have no good apart from you.' ...The LORD is my chosen portion and my cup; you hold my lot. The lines have fallen for me in pleasant places; indeed, I have a beautiful inheritance... Therefore my heart is glad, and my whole being rejoices... You make known to me the path of life; in your presence there is fullness of joy; at your right hand are pleasures forevermore.

Jesus echoed the sentiment of Psalm 16 when He prayed for us, "And this is eternal life, that they know you, the only true God, and Jesus Christ whom you have sent" (John 17:3). This is a striking statement. Eternal life is knowing the Lord. We may conceive of eternal life as something equal to heaven, a gift that begins when we die. Yet, this is a misunderstanding of the whole scope of man's original problem and God's gracious acts to fix it. The worst part about the death Adam suffered in the garden was separation from God. Accordingly, his spiritual death, which took the form of a heart of rebellion, cursed him to an inability to properly want God. As Paul wrote in Romans 1, the sinful man habitually trades God for lesser things. Man's separation from God and his hardened heart toward God are what desperately needed to be remedied. All that God has done in Christ to save us has not been about merely sparing us eternity in hell and giving us heaven, but has been about giving us HIM! In the gospel of Jesus Christ, we get God back!

His presence is what makes the new heaven and earth so heavenly, according to Revelation: "...Behold, the dwelling place of God is with man. He will dwell with them, and they will be his people, and God himself will be with them as their God" (Rev. 21:3b). You see, paradise is God with man. Marriage is our ultimate fulfillment, yet not an earthly marriage, but a heavenly marriage between a unified body of the redeemed and their Lord, Jesus Christ. The apostle Paul teaches that we've been given a down payment on this paradise in the form of the indwelling Spirit of Christ.[2] We enjoy a taste of the fulfillment of eternity now in the fellowship that the Spirit facilitates with God.

The numerous New Testament warnings against idolatry speak to the ongoing propensity even for believers to be pulled away by the search for fulfillment in things other than Him.[3] Human marriage—which we might call God's first gift (Gen. 2:20-25)—is one of the greatest gifts which we are tempted to value above the Giver. The testimony of Scripture and human experience from Genesis 3 to the present is that marriage, this wonderful gift, brings heartache into every life where it, rather than God, is sought as the ultimate fulfillment of the heart.

That this idolatry is so common is a terrible reality, but there is perhaps an even more egregious component. Christians bring God into their idolatry by praying that He'll deliver their idol to them. James 4:3 seems to indicate it's possible to pray for good things for the wrong reasons: "You ask and do not receive, because you ask wrongly, to spend it on your passions." When we pray that God will make our spouses love us the way we always wanted or even that He will "heal" our marriages, and *we do so from a desire that marriage would be our ultimate fulfillment*, we are guilty of idolatry.

Have you ever been tripped up by the atheist who asks, "Can God make a rock so big He can't lift it?" It's the old "omnipotence paradox." The argument goes that if you answer "yes" or "no" to the question, you've testified that God cannot be omnipotent—there is something God cannot do.[4] When we expect marriage to be our

---

[2] 2 Cor. 1:22, 5:5; Eph. 1:14

[3] 1 Cor. 10:7, 14; 2 Cor. 6:16; Eph. 5:5; Col. 3:5; 1 John 5:21

[4] The question is based upon a misunderstanding of the doctrine of omnipotence. That God is omnipotent does not mean that He can do anything, but that He can do

ultimate fulfillment and pray to God for that end, in a sense we are praying a similarly theologically ridiculous (and insulting) prayer: "God please give me something more wonderful than You." There is nothing more wonderful than God, and He has given Himself to us in Christ. To come to Him with such a request, implied or explicit, is to reject Him as our highest desire and joy and to ask Him to deliver something better, which is impossible.

It should be obvious why so many of us end up terribly disappointed or disillusioned in marriage. If ultimate satisfaction for the human heart can only be found in fellowship with God in Christ and we have traded that for something else, ultimate fulfillment cannot be found. Additionally, when we expect ultimate fulfillment from our spouses, we can only be disappointed as we place a God-sized expectation on them which they can never meet. Idols can only fail us. By reading the wrong music, we've sung a song that can never be beautiful.

The Song of Songs leads us to the right music. When we read it correctly, as would the apostles, we find that it depicts not only a love that we all want in marriage, but a love that believers already have received in Christ. It is the latter that is most prominent in the holy text.[5] Looking at the Song as a testimony of Christ's love for us will serve to correct our impulse to look for ultimate fulfillment in human marriage. With each text, we will be driven to consider the great self-sacrificial love of Jesus and His "pleasures forevermore" (Psa. 16:11). I truly believe that most believers, after reading the Song the way we will, will find it to be among the most Christ-exalting devotional material in the Bible. Further, we will see just how crucial it is to the success of our marriages to value Him above all things, including our marriages.

---

anything that is consistent with His character. The Scriptures give us numerous things that God cannot do. For example, God cannot lie, change His mind, or deny Himself (Num. 23:19; Tit. 1:2 [literally, "the unlying God"]; 2 Tim. 2:13). None of these inabilities indicate He is less than all-powerful. For God to make a rock so big He could not lift it would require Him to do something illogical, which is contrary to His nature. The laws of logic originate in the mind of God. What we call the law of non-contradiction is the character of "the unlying God" reflected in His creation.

[5] A case will be made for this statement in the next chapter.

The Wrong Key

When I was in high school, I was cast in a local review of Broadway show tunes. They put me in "Do You Hear the People Sing?" from *Les Miserables*. My role was to march onto the stage by myself and begin the song *a capella*. After the first line, another cast member was to join me and begin singing. Then another, and another, until five or six of us were standing on the stage singing *a capella*. About seven lines in, the band was to join us for a rousing finish.

One small problem. I don't have perfect pitch, and the previous song was in a different key. The night of the first show, I marched onto the stage singing "Do You Hear the People Sing?" in the key of the previous song, which was a half-step lower. My fellow singers joined me on stage, following my lead in the wrong key. When the band came in playing the appropriate key…well, let's just say that the second line of the song— "singing the song of angry men"—turned out to be prophetic. It sounded worse than awful, and the next night of the show I was given the task of being the *second* person to enter the stage.

Dissonance. It's a musical term for when notes clash with one another. It's the opposite of harmony. We could say that it is also descriptive of marriages founded on the belief that fulfillment comes from someone meeting our expectations and needs. "It is better to give than receive" may be embroidered on a jillion throw pillows, but it is written on relatively few hearts. Many of us do come to marriage enthralled with the idea of having someone to love, but most of the heartache comes from not being loved enough. The husband and wife each want something they are not getting, and the mutual pursuit of self leads to a battle wherein dissonance is the tragic norm.

Some reading this may reject that idea, believing that most people have a decent view of love, that love is about giving rather than receiving. Yet, knowing and doing are two completely different things. How many marriages are you aware of that have ended in divorce because one or both spouses were frustrated by too few opportunities to serve? How many husbands and wives do you know whose great heartache is that their spouse won't allow them to give enough? On the contrary, the typical issues in marriage arise from unmet expectations— "You are supposed to meet my needs, and you haven't done it."

Desire for self-fulfillment and aversion to self-sacrifice are even evidenced in changes in wedding vows in recent decades. It used to be "as long as we both shall *live*." Now, it's not uncommon to hear, "as long as we both shall *love*." Even that alteration doesn't accurately reflect the hearts of many husbands and wives. It would be more honest to say, "as long as we both love...me."

This is an ancient tune. This tendency to seek self comes straight out of the curses uttered by God in Genesis 3. It's already been noted that marriage could be considered God's first gift. It didn't take long for man to use it for self-fulfillment and wreak havoc on mankind. In Genesis 2, God gave this wonderful gift along with a brief indication of how it should work. The husband should lovingly lead and care for his wife. The wife should respectfully submit to her husband. That was God's design for this good gift— evidence that He intended it to reflect His relationship with His people.[6]

The moment the man and woman rejected God's design, they took the gift for themselves and began to use it for their own ends. If we carefully read the narrative of Genesis 3, we notice that the serpent, the man, and the woman ignored God's design. The serpent spoke not to the man as God had done but spoke exclusively to the woman. The wife led; the husband followed.[7] For selfish gain, the wife disregarded her husband's instruction, which he received from the Lord.[8] From what appears to be the worst of morbid curiosity—perhaps wondering, "What will happen to her?"—the husband merely watched

---

[6] If you read Genesis 2, you may wonder, "Where is he getting this stuff about the husband leading and the wife submitting?" We get it from Paul. A major premise of this book is that we should read the Old Testament as did the New Testament authors. When we do that with Genesis 2–3, we come to the conclusions that Paul outlines in 1 Corinthians 11:3–9 and 1 Timothy 2:11–14. He derives God's intention from the facts that Adam was formed first, then Eve; Eve was made from Adam; and Eve was made for Adam.

[7] Genesis 3:6 notes that the man was with the woman during the temptation. He did nothing. He did not fulfill his role as leader and protector. That this was an offense against God is clear from the words spoken to Adam in 3:17, "<u>Because you have listened to the voice of your wife</u> and have eaten of the tree..."

[8] Gen. 3:6

as his wife walked headlong into destruction. Both rejected their roles and responsibility toward one another and thereby rejected God. As a result, the selfish impulse that motivated them in those moments became hardwired into their hearts; for God said to the woman, "Your desire shall be for your husband, and he shall rule over you" (Gen. 3:16).

"Your desire shall be for your husband" points to a desire to dominate. The same verb is used one chapter later when God warned Cain about sin, "Its *desire* is for you, but you must rule over it" (Gen. 4:7). It's an obscure Hebrew verb, used only three times in the whole Old Testament, two of them in tight proximity in Genesis 3–4. Clearly, this is not a *loving* desire, but a desire to dominate. Just as sin desired to dominate Cain, the natural tendency of a wife would be to dominate her husband, to usurp his authority for her own ends. Conversely, her husband would "rule over" her. He would abuse his authority, either by being harshly domineering or by being carelessly passive, as Adam was earlier in the chapter.

Terrible things resulted from Adam and Eve's sin, not the least of which is that husbands and wives are naturally bent to seek self over spouse. Read the following narrative in the book of Genesis alone and you will see it over and over with devastating consequences.

Believers are still tempted by their old nature.[9] If dissonant self-seeking exists between a husband and wife, the curse is still alive and well. They are singing the same song, but in the absolute wrong key.

The Song of Songs leads us to the right key. It shows the love of Christ for us, His bride, and how this love enables us to love like He does. If we then apply the book as would the apostles, we will move to emulate His love in our marriages. Christ exemplifies the ideal love depicted in each section of the Song. Faithfulness to Him requires us to follow His self-sacrificial, passionate, potently monogamous example of love. The Song leads us to delight in Him and to delight in being like Him as we love our spouses well.

---

[9] This is why Paul gives direct instruction in Ephesians 5 about how to love one another well as spouses. The husband is to give himself up for his wife; the wife is to submit to and respect her husband.

Faithfulness Demands a Beautiful Song

Because Christ is our ultimate fulfillment, does this mean that human marriage is intended to be less than pleasurable? Is it wrong to desire fulfillment in marriage? The answer to both questions is a resounding, "No!" On the contrary, when we understand the New Testament teaching on marriage, we see that a godly marriage must be pleasurable and fulfilling.

The gospel is precisely what human marriage is intended to depict. The instruction to husbands is specifically, "Love your wives, as Christ loved the church and gave himself up for her" (Eph. 5:25). To the wife, Paul writes, "Wives, submit to your own husbands, as to the Lord. For the husband is the head of the wife even as Christ is the head of the church..." (Eph. 5:22–23a). This arrangement is not merely a return to God's Genesis 2 design, but it is also an evangelistic tool of God. You see, at the end of all his instruction on marriage, Paul ends with this: "This mystery is profound, and I am saying that it refers to Christ and the church" (Eph. 5:32). The union of a husband and wife is intended to serve as a flesh-and-blood picture of the *other-centered* relationship between Jesus Christ and the church. Marriage was invented to display the glory of redemption, wherein a loving Savior gave all that He is for His bride, and she lovingly surrenders to Him as Lord.

Like a dye that leaves its imprint on impressionable metal, so the union of Christ and the church is the original stamp, intended to leave its mark on Christian marriage, so that when the world looks at Christian marriage, it sees a clear picture of Christ and the church. By the grace of God, there is something glorious that happens when marriage is exactly that—it is unquenchably passionate and fulfilling. When we understand this, we see that our marriages *must* be fulfilling if they are to be faithful imprints of Christ and the church. It dishonors God to settle for a joyless, passionless, unfulfilling, and therefore, gospel-defaming marriage.

However, our marriages can be truly fulfilling and mirror Christ only if they have self-sacrificial love at the foundation. Christ did not love His church by saying, "What have you done for me lately?" Instead, He first loved His bride and gave Himself up for her. That is marriage as God intended.

It's ironic that people find Paul's instruction on marriage to be a burdensome thing. It's not! It's downright glorious. Our ultimate fulfillment comes from enjoying this self-sacrificial love with Christ. Secondarily and out of faithfulness to Him, we are fulfilled as we mirror this love in our marriages. By God's design, it is all intensely pleasurable.

A gospel-defaming marriage—unfulfilling, joyless, passionless—should grieve us because it lies about the gospel. This should motivate us to change more than anything. The surrounding world watches Christian husbands and wives to see if the gospel they proclaim really does what they say it does. What a tragedy if rather than demonstrating a marriage that commends the gospel, pointing others to the passionate, eternal fellowship between Christ and the church, our marriages look just like all the Christ-less marriages of our unsaved friends, neighbors, and co-workers. The watching world is left with no option but to conclude that the gospel is nonsense.

There are two components to singing the song God has written. First, we must enjoy the gospel that He has sung in Christ. Second, we must sing it just like Him in our marriages so that the gospel will be commended to the world. Where do we find the sheet music? The most beautiful rendition is found in the Song of Songs.

The Greatest Song

The Song of Songs is the ideal text for us in this because it depicts marital love as God intended, exemplified by Christ. It elevates our hearts in affection for Him, which serves to correct our tendency to seek ultimate fulfillment in other loves. It points to Him as the perfect example of love, which prods us toward His brand of self-sacrificial love.

If we learn to sing the Song, we will see that no one could love us as thoroughly and as well as Jesus. No earthly marriage could bring the fullness of joy that comes at His side. Ironically, this will position us to value and serve our spouses appropriately. If we learn to sing the Song, we'll become like Jesus, a self-sacrificial, beloved Giver. By our marriages we will then declare to the world, "Look at this kind of love—only the gospel can do this."

Discussion Questions/Activities

The questions/activities at the end of each chapter are intended to be useful to individuals, couples, and small groups. Please modify them to fit your needs.

1. How would you describe your expectations of marriage prior to your wedding? In what ways have those expectations been met? How has your marriage fallen short of those expectations?

2. If you could change one thing about your marriage, what would it be?

3. What specific things have you done to try to invigorate or repair your marriage?

4. What influence have the Scriptures and prayer had on your marriage?

5. Is the idea of marriage as a picture of the gospel a new concept to you? How might this change your perspective on the current state of your marriage?

6. Read the Song of Songs, if possible, in one sitting. What are your initial thoughts? Fantasy, or attainable reality?

02

THE GREATEST SONG

"The Song of Songs, which is Solomon's…" (Song 1:1)
Attitudes about and dispositions toward the Song of Songs will be diverse, depending upon our different backgrounds. A friend recently told me, "When I was a kid, we only had 65 books in our Bible. We pretended the Song of Solomon wasn't there!" Not many people know what to do with the Song because not many people know how to understand it. Beyond its interpretational challenges, for many it's just uncomfortably sexual. However, a careful reading will reveal glorious things, repairing our wrong thinking about marriage, and leading eventually to what we have wanted all along—a more passionate, meaningful relationship with our spouse.

Before we launch into the first section, it would be wise to get a lay of the land. It may surprise some to learn that a literal reading of the Song as a celebration of human romance and sexuality is a relatively late development. Church scholars have written voluminously on the Song since the time of Christ and the vast majority of those writings interpreted the Song *Christologically*. What does that mean? It means that they understood the Song to refer in some sense to the mystery of the relationship between Christ and the Church. That has been the majority position for most church history.

It is only in the last approximately 200 years that interpreters have taken a more literal approach, understanding the Song to be a straightforward celebration of romantic and sexual human love. Most modern Christians, who have only ever read the Song in this literal fashion, are unaware that this is almost a novelty when considered in the entire scope of Jewish and Christian history.

I'll argue below for a Christological understanding of the Song. I would agree with the preponderance of our forefathers that this greatest of songs must have the greatest of bridegrooms at its center. However, I would go further than most of them by saying that while it is correct to see Christ as the center of the Song, if we would read and apply the Song as would the biblical authors, we *must* apply it to marriage. It seems to me that much of what the greats of church history wrote regarding Christ as the great lover of the Song can and should be emulated by husbands and wives in Christian marriage. Given what Paul teaches about the mystery of marriage in Ephesians 5:22–33, I believe this is not only reasonable, but is intended by the Holy Spirit.

Therefore, our approach will be unique in that we will follow the text *through Christ* to Christian marriage.[1] With each section, we will follow the story of the text as a picture of divine love. Then we will consider how the love depicted is exemplified by Christ. That exemplified love will then be applied to marriage. Again, the rationale for this is the conviction that this is how the apostles would read and apply the Song. More will be said about this shortly.

This book is intended to be intensely Christ-centered. It has as its object not just fixing bad marriages. Jesus is so lovely, so compelling, so desirable, that if this Song has its way in us, His gentle aroma about our necks (Song 1:12–14) will soothe our hearts in the wake of a marriage that may *not* be fixed. The greatest result of this

---

[1] I am not suggesting that there are no modern books or commentaries that simultaneously find Christ at the center of the Song and make valid application to marriage. I could name several fine works that do. However, I have found that each work typically presents one as a primary objective while tacking on the other in a distracting, disjointed way. For example, there are commentaries that give very helpful application to marriage, but when it comes time to connect the text to Christ, that connection seems to come out of left field. The comments about Christ either are not driven by the text itself or bear little resemblance to what was written about marriage. It is almost as if two different commentaries were being written—one about the Song from a literal perspective, and one from a Christological perspective. On the other hand, some books do very well interpreting the book Christologically, but the application to marriage seems somewhat unrelated to the comments about Christ.

study would be for all to say first and foremost, not of our spouses, but of Christ, "This is my beloved and this is my friend" (Song 5:16). Any benefit to our marriages will flow from that. When both a husband and a wife find their greatest treasure in Him, that is when divine love is possible in human marriage. If any text should speak to those who would love well, it should be the picture of love exemplified by our Great Bridegroom in the Greatest Song.

A Song About Divine, Marital Love

The first verse tells us we are reading a song: "The Song of Songs, which is Solomon's." In other words, this is poetry, which means that we will handle it differently than we would other genres of Scripture, such as historical narrative or prophecy. It does tell a story, but not like a typical narrative. It uses poetic language, evoking emotion. It is intended to stir us up. It may not be primarily about conveying information. For that reason, we cannot study the Song of Songs the same way we study Romans. Different genres communicate differently and they do different things.

To illustrate the point, let's look at a few lines of the Song. Then we'll consider what might be a faithful prose version of those lines.[2]

(He)[3]
I came to my garden, my sister, my bride,
I gathered my myrrh with my spice,
I ate my honeycomb with my honey,
I drank my wine with my milk.

---

[2] Douglas Sean O'Donnell makes a similar demonstration using a secular poem in his very practical commentary. Douglas Sean O'Donnell, *The Song of Solomon: An Invitation to Intimacy*, Preaching the Word (Wheaton, Illinois: Crossway, 2012), 18.

[3] Modern translations add headings to indicate who is speaking in the Song. For example, the ESV divides the text into paragraphs and adds the headings, "She," "Others," and "He." These headings are based upon the gender and number of the Hebrew words in the original text. However, in many cases, the Hebrew text is not conclusive and the context must be the determining factor. This is why translations and commentators at times differ regarding who is speaking. In this book, such headings represent my understanding of the text and are not taken from the ESV.

(Chorus)
Eat, friends, drink, and be drunk with love![4]

Now the prose version:

(He)
I had sex with my wife.

(Chorus)
Proceed!

Does the prose version say the same thing as the poetic version? Kind of. But when you hear the poem first, it seems almost criminal to just strip it down to the information. These two genres do different things in the reader. The latter imparts information. The former imparts longing.

The Song of Songs is intended to impart longing. If we take it apart like we would Romans, going immediately to grammatical nuts and bolts, we will miss what the Song is intended to do, which is to make us long for something. It's a song.

It's a song about *divine* love. It depicts the kind of love of which, in a fallen world, only God is naturally capable. It comes from Him. It belongs to Him. He naturally loves this way and if any others would love this way, they will have to be empowered by Him. It is divine love.

It's a song about divine, *marital* love. Clearly, the Song is about a husband and wife, and clearly it is sexual. If you have ever read the Song, you will agree. I have chosen the word "marital" instead of "sexual" because the love depicted is not only sexual. The man and woman of the Song desire one another in every way. They have given themselves to one another completely—their whole persons, not just their bodies.

Yet, their bodies are included. Marriage, as God intended it, is inherently sexual. Sexuality is the physical expression of the totality of the intimacy of marriage, the physical pleasure that comes from the

---

[4] Song 5:1

uniting of two entire beings. When two people have given themselves to one another in total monogamous commitment, free to be completely vulnerable, sharing their hearts, their futures, their service—that is when sexual intimacy is explosively pleasurable. It's the physical culmination of sharing everything they are. The more they share of themselves, the better that physical culmination will be.

If this is a song that tells a story of divine, marital love, what exactly is that storyline? Many commentators believe it's about the engagement of a man and woman; the building excitement before the wedding; the consummation of their marriage on the wedding night; a lover's quarrel, followed by a reconciliation; and the bliss of more physical and emotional intimacy.[5] I will make the case that this is a story about two people who are already married. They enjoy their marital prerogatives from the very beginning of the Song. I agree that there is a lover's quarrel and reconciliation, but this takes place between a husband and wife, not a man and his betrothed. More importantly, the Song is an idealized love story within a marriage. It's a married couple who are nuts about each other.

It is idealized, not idealistic. It is love as God intended, but not a love that is out of reach for those who belong to Christ. The Song evokes Eden. The garden imagery is overwhelming. A robust understanding of the gospel is that Christ returns to us what was lost in Eden. This has glorious implications for those wondering, "Is this all there is?"

What's Solomon Got to Do with It?

Given that most of us have always known this book as "The Song of Solomon," some obvious questions are in order. What is Solomon's role? Is he the main character? Is he the author? Among conservative evangelical scholars there is no widespread agreement on these questions, even on the question of whether Solomon wrote this song.

Let's consider Solomon's role within the song. He is a character; no one denies this—he is mentioned multiple times. But is

---

[5] It is not my intention to caricature the views with which I do not agree. I have tried not to do so with this sentence. This summary is necessarily brief and simple—if not simplistic—in its attempt to cover a multitude of commentaries holding a wide range of nuanced understanding of the Song.

he the husband depicted? There are good reasons to believe that he is not. Neither the text of the Song itself nor biblical writings outside the Song support the idea that Solomon is the husband of the Song.

We know from Scriptures outside the Song that Solomon's love life was disastrous. The first remark made to this effect is in 1 Kings 3:1a: "Solomon made a marriage alliance with Pharaoh king of Egypt. He took Pharaoh's daughter and brought her into the city of David..." This cannot be explained away as political expediency. It was disobedience to God's law, and it got much worse, as we see in 1 Kings 11:1–4:

> Now King Solomon loved many foreign women, along with the daughter of Pharaoh: Moabite, Ammonite, Edomite, Sidonian, and Hittite women, from the nations concerning which the LORD had said to the people of Israel, "You shall not enter into marriage with them, neither shall they with you, for surely they will turn away your heart after their gods." Solomon clung to these in love. He had 700 wives, who were princesses, and 300 concubines. And his wives turned away his heart. For when Solomon was old his wives turned away his heart after other gods, and his heart was not wholly true to the LORD his God, as was the heart of David his father.

If you have read the Song of Songs, you can see what a stretch it is to view Solomon as the monogamous, committed, nuts-about-a-Jewish-shepherdess husband depicted there. If he is the husband of the Song, then within the larger context of Scripture we are forced to understand him to be saying to the woman in the Song, "I literally have a thousand sexual partners...but, Baby, you're my favorite!" It doesn't work. Solomon is the Bible's poster boy for how not to do marriage.

Solomon's disastrous love life is precisely why he is in the Song, but not as the husband. The Song presents him as a foil for the monogamous love of the husband and wife. That is, his presence in the story represents a contrast to the love exhibited by this husband and wife, highlighting how unique and wonderful their love is.

But did Solomon write the Song? Is that what we should gather from the first verse: "The Song of Songs, which is Solomon's"? There are a number of ways to take that last clause. The Hebrew text is slightly ambiguous. It could be read, "which is *to* Solomon" or "which is *for* Solomon" or "which *belongs to* Solomon" or "which is *about* Solomon." So he could have written it, or someone else could have written it to, or for, or about him.

It makes most sense to hold that Solomon wrote this Song. There are several reasons. First, we know that Solomon was a prolific author. 1 Kings 4:32 tells us that he spoke 3,000 proverbs and wrote 1,005 songs. Second, it doesn't make sense that someone else would write this *for* or *to* Solomon. How would you present a gift like that? "Here, King Solomon. I have a gift for you. It's a song about idealized love. You play a very important role. Your disastrous love life is the darkness against which the blissful marital love of the main characters shines. You're welcome." It is likely that the average Israelite under Solomon had more sense than that.

But why would Solomon write such a thing about himself? That leads to a third reason to support his authorship. Solomon very honestly appraised his own failings in love elsewhere in Scripture. This is implied in Proverbs, especially chapters 5–7. "Don't go after the forbidden woman! Trust me!" The "trust me" part is not in there, but when you know what is written about him in 1 Kings 11, you know that at least some of the wisdom in Proverbs was acquired the hard way.

Solomon's honesty regarding his failings in love is clearer in Ecclesiastes. In chapter 2, he wrote, "I kept my heart from no pleasure...and behold, all was vanity" (Eccl. 2:10–11). In 7:26, he wrote, "And I find something more bitter than death: the woman whose heart is snares and nets, and whose hands are fetters. He who pleases God escapes her, but the sinner is taken by her." You can hear the echoes of 1 Kings 11. Solomon acknowledges, "I've learned the hard way about what love is and isn't supposed to be." Solomon did not have an idealized picture of his own love life. He was honest about it. He was honest about it in Ecclesiastes. It makes sense that he's the best person to be honest about it in the Song of Songs.

In the Song, Solomon writes as an utter failure at love, basically saying, "Don't be like me. There's something so much better."

Exemplified by Christ

This is a song about divine, marital love…exemplified by Christ. It should be read Christologically. That is, it should be read through the New Testament lens of the coming of Jesus Christ[6], as somehow pointing to Him. There are several reasons for this.

First, Jesus read the whole Old Testament Christologically. Remember Jesus on the road to Emmaus with the two disciples just after His resurrection? In Luke 24:27, we find, "And beginning with Moses and all the Prophets, [Jesus] interpreted to them in all the Scriptures the things concerning himself." Are we to believe that there should be an understood footnote there, saying, "Well, not all the Scriptures. All the Scriptures except the Song of Songs"? No, Jesus interpreted to the disciples in *all* the Scriptures the things concerning Himself. Similarly, in John 5:39, Jesus said, "You search the Scriptures because you think that in them you have eternal life; and it is they that bear witness about me." All the Scriptures testify about Jesus.

Second, the title itself indicates something more than mere human marriage. There are many songs and poems in the Bible, but this song is called *the Song of Songs*, which is the Hebrew way of saying, "the very best song," or "the greatest song." Would the Bible—a book about all that God has done to glorify Himself by redeeming a people through the death, resurrection, and exaltation of His Son—call a song that is merely about human marriage, "the greatest song?" Not likely.

Third, marriage was a primary metaphor used by the Holy Spirit to depict the relationship between God and His people in the Old Testament. The theme of God as husband and Israel as bride is all

---

[6] This may be difficult for some to comprehend, especially considering the somewhat graphic sexual imagery in the Song. We may find the idea troubling, but as previously mentioned, the vast majority of interpreters in the history of the church had no problem with understanding Christ as central to the Song, even in the sexual passages. That's because they understood that the Grand Author of Scripture chose sexual language because sexual union is the most pleasurable of human experiences; it is ecstasy. Therefore, it is the perfect metaphor in the human experience for the wonder of fellowship with Christ. Fellowship with Jesus is the highest of pleasures (Psa. 16:11). Similarly, the Bible frequently describes idolatry as adultery, using very graphic terms (Exo. 34:15; Lev. 17:7; Jdg. 8:33; Jer. 2:23–24, 5:7–8, 13:26–27; Eze. 23:3; Hos. 2:2). All of this is biblical language, and we need to be okay with biblical language.

over the Old Testament.[7] Does it make sense that in the premier marriage song of the Bible, that theme would be absent? No.

Fourth, the text of the song itself has Christological pointers. The husband in the poem is a shepherd king! More important is what we read in Song 8:6: "Set me as a seal upon your heart, as a seal upon your arm, for love is strong as death, jealousy is fierce as the grave. Its flashes are flashes of fire, the very flame of the LORD." The passion of love is the very flame of Yahweh! All this passion we read about in the Song—it comes from Him. It's His.

Fifth, the New Testament authors read the Old Testament Christologically. They understood the entirety of the Old Testament to point toward Christ via prophecies, types, and shadows.[8] For example, in 1 Corinthians 10 Paul writes that the rock from which the Israelites drank in the wilderness was Christ (v4). Just a few verses later the apostle adds, "We must not put *Christ* to the test, as some of them did and were destroyed by serpents" (v9). You can check out the story in Numbers 21. The Israelites grumbled against Yahweh, and He sent fiery serpents to bite them, killing a multitude. Yet, according to Paul, who did they test? Christ.

In Hebrews, we are told that Moses "considered the reproach of *Christ* greater wealth than the treasures of Egypt" (Heb. 11:26). Indeed, the whole book of Hebrews is based upon the premise that the Old Testament points forward to Jesus. While the Song itself is never quoted in the New Testament, there is evidence in Hebrews that if it had been, it would be understood Christologically. Psalm 45 is a marriage psalm. If you take the time to read the Song of Songs and then Psalm 45, you will be struck by the similarities. Significantly, the author of Hebrews quotes Psalm 45, applying it to Jesus.[9]

Not only do the New Testament authors read the Old Testament Christologically, but the New Testament repeatedly characterizes Jesus as a bridegroom. John the Baptist calls Jesus "the bridegroom"

---

[7] Just a smattering of references in the prophets: Eze. 16:7–8; Jer. 2:2, 19–20; Isa. 54:5–8, 62:5

[8] Col. 2:16–17; Heb. 7–10

[9] Heb. 1:8–9: But of the Son he says, "Your throne, O God, is forever and ever, the scepter of uprightness is the scepter of your kingdom. You have loved righteousness and hated wickedness; therefore God, your God, has anointed you with the oil of gladness beyond your companions."

in John 3:29.[10] Paul wrote in 2 Corinthians 11:2, "For I feel a divine jealousy for you, since I betrothed you to one husband, to present you as a pure virgin to Christ." Likewise, the consummation of the kingdom at the second coming is depicted as a wedding feast, as in Matthew 22:2 and Revelation 19:7. How can we read of *the* ideal marriage and bridegroom in the Song of Songs and not be intended by the Holy Spirit to think of Christ?

Perhaps the most obvious reason to believe that the New Testament authors would read the Song Christologically is the passage in Ephesians 5:22–33, where Paul gives instruction to husbands and wives based upon the example of Christ and the church. The end of that passage is particularly striking: "'Therefore a man shall leave his father and mother and hold fast to his wife, and the two shall become one flesh.' This mystery is profound, and I am saying that it refers to Christ and the church" (Eph. 5:31–32). The mystery of marriage between a man and a woman, Paul writes, refers to Christ and the church. In other words, Paul is unable to think about the institution of marriage without thinking about Jesus and His bride. It is not simply that Christ and the church are the example that husbands and wives are to follow. Rather, all husbands and wives are a picture pointing to Christ and the church. Human marriage is a copy; Christ and the church is the original.

The Old Testament can only be rightly understood in light of the New Testament. We can and should study a book taking into consideration its genre, historical context, and context within the canon. However, one cannot fully understand or apply an Old Testament book outside of the revelation of Jesus Christ. Jesus casts the fullest light on the books of the Old Testament,[11] and certainly on the Song of Songs. This is why the *vast* majority of books and commentaries on this Old Testament book have read it in light of Christ.

---

[10] cf Matt. 9:14–15
[11] Luke 24: 27; Col. 2:17

Reading the Song in Light of Christ

As we study each section of the Song, we will first try to understand the story of the Song itself. What is the Song saying about the man and the woman and their love? Then we will consider how Christ exemplifies that love. We will do this before attempting to apply anything to our own marriages. This approach is what makes this book unique among books on the Song and marriage books in general. As the preceding section has shown, the biblical authors would almost certainly understand this greatest of songs to have a primarily Christological focus. However, following Paul's lead (Eph. 5:22–33), we will naturally seek to emulate the way Christ exemplifies the love of the Song. If we skip the crucial step of considering how Christ exemplifies the love of the Song, going straight to applying the love of the Song to our marriages, we risk failure.

"I can't do this!"

What do many of us think when we read the Song, this idealized picture of marital love, without Christ in mind? "I can't do that! I can't love someone who is imperfect as if they were perfect! I can't enjoy ecstatic passion with someone who has hurt me! I can't be so perfectly virtuous and therefore irresistibly desirable that my spouse would risk life and limb to pursue me into the darkness!" We come to the Song and say, "This is impossible! I can't do this. I can't be this."

The natural man is right to think that way. The Fall completely twisted up the beautiful Edenic union of a man and a woman. Sin entered their hearts in such a way that they are bent against one another in mutual self-seeking. It's part of the curse itself for them to struggle against one another, to contend with one another.[12] We see this playing out in the narrative of the Old Testament. We see it playing out in history, on the news, in our family lives growing up, and in our own homes today. We can't do this. We can't be this.

---

[12] Gen. 3:16

"He can!"

The Holy Spirit, the grand author of Scripture, shows us One who can, who has, who does and is—Jesus Christ, the righteous, the Bridegroom. Jesus gives Himself completely to His bride—He did this on the cross, pouring out His blood to make her His. He has withheld nothing of Himself from her. He has loved her as if she were flawless even though she is not. He's like the husband in the Song.

And though we fail Him, though we sin against Him, He eagerly reconciles with us and enjoys passionate fellowship with us. No matter how many times we wrong Him, He forgives and gives Himself to us. He considers Himself ours. He's like the husband in the Song.

And Jesus is so perfectly loving and virtuous that those who belong to Him are willing to pursue Him into the night, risking all, risking life and limb to follow Him. All of church history has demonstrated this as countless thousands have walked to the gallows and have been burned at the stake, all to know greater fellowship with this ultimately desirable Bridegroom—so desirable is He! He is like the husband in the Song.

He pours himself out to make us His and to make Himself ours. The gospel gives such rich meaning to the words of this Song. "My beloved is mine, and I am his" (Song 2:16). "This is my beloved and this is my friend" (Song 5:16). Jesus is like the husband of the Song.

This is not to say that the husband in the song *is* Jesus. The husband is an idealized husband who loves with a divine love. Jesus loves better than the husband in the Song. This love is *exemplified* by Jesus. He is the ultimate fulfillment of this love…and He empowers others to live this way.

The portions of this book in which we will consider the love of Christ will be the most valuable and practical. They will warm our hearts toward the Lord Jesus, causing us to desire to be like Him. They will fuel our desire to emulate Him in our marriages. And by considering His love in the gospel, we will be continually reminded not only that His love motivates us to become like Him, but it enables us to become like Him.

Emulated by Husbands And Wives

Jesus not only exemplifies the love of the Song, but He fixes us so that we can love like the Song. What fantastic news to the one asking, "Is this all there is?" The brokenness of the Fall is reversed in Christ! That is what Ephesians 2:1–10 teaches. We were dead in trespasses and sins. Enslaved to sinful passions. Enslaved to living for ourselves, the devil, and the world. But in that passage, Paul offers a world of hope to all the broken, including you who are living in passionless marriages, filled with unreconciled hurt. God rescued us in Christ and raised us to live differently. He rescued us from the penalty and the power of our sin, so that we could live differently in this life.

Verse 10 teaches that He created us in Christ for good works. Just three chapters later, in Ephesians 5, Paul teaches that among those works is the ability to live as husband and wife *as do Christ and the church*. That's right. Christ exemplifies the love of the Song, and according to Ephesians, He empowers us to emulate Him. Because of the Ephesians 2 gospel, we are enabled and called to emulate Christ and the church in our marriages.

Only believers can do this because only believers have been rescued from the curse and the havoc it wreaks on human relationships. With the gospel at work in us, the Holy Spirit would take us back to the Song and perhaps say, "You see this kind of love that loves another as if she were flawless even though she is not? This love that forgives even when it has been wronged? You see this kind of lover who is so virtuous and delightful that the spouse is drawn irresistibly to pursue the other at risk of life and limb? *You* are capable of being that and doing that because Christ has dedicated Himself from His ascension to His second coming to sanctifying you. You are able to be this, and when you commit yourself to it, it is *delightful*. Just look at the man and woman of the Song."

Believers not only can live the love of the Song, they are obligated to do so. 2 Corinthians 5:15 reads, "And he died for all, that those who live might no longer live for themselves but for him who for their sake died and was raised." Jesus did not save you so you could go your own way and do your own thing. He saved you to be

His. You exist for His purpose. Further, your marriage belongs to Him. You do not have the right to settle for a miserable marriage. You do not have the right to have a passionless marriage. Your marriage is God's and He wants it to burn with mutual pleasure—not merely sexual pleasure—but mutual pleasure that comes from enjoying one another in every way.

The gospel we proclaim fixes the mess the Fall made of marriage. When believers are content with worldly marriages where years of hurt stifle passion, vulnerability, and joy, they live like those who are still in Adam. They defame the gospel. To paraphrase Titus 1:16, they claim to know God, but they deny Him with their marriages! May it never be.

Your marriage should demonstrate the truth of the gospel you proclaim. People around you should look at your marriage and say, "These two people adore each other in spite of how they've hurt each other and in spite of their physical and non-physical imperfections. How is that possible in a world where marriages can't seem to stay together, and if they do, they turn into lifelong cold wars? …Oh, the gospel must be true."

Conversely, a loveless, passionless marriage, riddled with bitterness—what does that say to those around you about the gospel you proclaim? It says, "The gospel is nonsense. It obviously hasn't changed them. They're just like everyone else."

Jesus rescued us from our sin and death and imminent wrath. With the Song of Songs, He wants to rescue us from miserable, gospel-denying marriages. He wants to take us to something better, not by calling us to pretend something, but by calling us to believe the gospel and live it out with one another.

What the Song Expects of Us

The Song calls us to passionate fellowship with Christ. The Song calls us to enjoy the reality of our belonging to Jesus and His belonging to us.

The Song calls us to passionate fellowship in our marriages. It calls us to commend the gospel by enjoying the same passionate giving and receiving in our marriages that we see in the marriage of Christ and His bride.

Passion for Christ. Passion in marriage. Let us give ourselves to this.

Discussion Questions/Activities

1. Read the Song of Songs, if possible, in one sitting. Upon this second reading, do you see any words, phrases, or ideas repeated in the Song?

2. After reading the Song, in what ways does it seem natural to understand it as pointing ultimately to Jesus? In what ways does it seem odd?

3. Read Ephesians 5:22–33. How might Paul's teaching on marriage inform the way that we interpret the Song?

4. Why is it so essential to read the Song Christologically? What bearing does this have on our application of the Song to marriage?

03

LONGING

The Pull of Companionship

Some parents dread having "the talk" with their kids, considering it among the most awkward conversations of life. My wife and I may be weirdos, but we relished the opportunity to prevent the culture from setting the narrative in our kids' minds and hearts regarding this wonderful gift of God. We have three sons and two daughters. We agreed early on that when the time came for each of them, I would handle the boys, while she would handle the girls.

They didn't all take the news the same way. One of the boys was completely unfazed, as if I had just explained tax law. Another sat silently, catatonic. One of the girls covered her mouth and replied, "Oh, it's just so DISTURBING!" Yet, they all had one thing in common. Eventually, the lightbulb came on and they realized what this meant about Mom and Dad. All five asked some variation of the same question: "So you and mom did that...*five times?*"

Their incredulity was priceless, and yet it made sense. At the time we dropped the bomb on each of them, they lacked the hormonal influence to make the whole thing sound like a good idea. Try stepping back into the shoes of a pre-pubescent child hearing this kind of news and imagine that no hormones are going to come to the eventual rescue. If you remove the blessings of sex drive and sexual fulfillment from the equation, you would be right to be somewhat reluctant about such an undertaking. When it came to human sexuality, God knew what He was doing on numerous levels. Without the natural desire for sexual fulfillment that comes later in life, procreation would be like an extremely awkward chore and the human race would likely disappear. Desire draws us to fulfillment.

We can see the same principle at work in our need for food and drink. Our bodies need food in order to survive, but imagine how monotonous and burdensome the task of nourishing ourselves would be without both the physical sensation of hunger and the satisfaction of fullness. Keeping our bodies fueled would be a simple matter of self-discipline. Our bodies long for nutrition and hydration and we receive pleasure from following that desire. How kind of God to give us taste buds in our mouths and neurons lining our digestive system so that it is pleasurable to eat and drink!

These physical passions are not the only ways that God leads us to fulfillment. He has also put into our hearts a desire for companionship. One of many ways in which we are made in the image of God is that we are communal beings.

The existence of God, as the Trinity, teaches us that God is a communal being. Read the book of John. Jesus repeatedly refers to the special relationship He has with the Father, a relationship of mutual love, which existed before the foundation of the world.[1] The Spirit is so relationally close to the other two members of the Trinity that He is referred to as both the Spirit of Christ and the Spirit of God.[2] Their relationship is not only characterized by love, but They delight to be of the same mind.[3]

Made in His image, we too derive pleasure from companionship. Ultimately, we derive the greatest relational pleasure from joining in the fellowship of the Trinity! Yes, Jesus prayed for us on the night before His crucifixion:

---

[1] John 3:35, 5:20, 8:42, 10:17, 14:31, 15:10, 17:23–24

[2] Gen 1:2; Exo. 31:3; 1 Sam. 10:10; Job 33:4; Matt. 3:16; Acts 16:7; Rom. 8:8–9, 14; 1 Cor. 2:11, 12:3; Eph. 4:30; Phil. 1:19; 1 Pet. 1:11

[3] Matt. 12:28; John 4:34, 8:28–29, 14:26, 16:13–15; Rom. 8:27; 1 Cor. 2:10–11; 1 John 4:2–3

I do not ask for these only, but also for those who will believe in me through their word, that they may all be one, just as you, Father, are in me, and I in you, that they also may be in us…I in them and you in me, that they may become perfectly one, so that the world may know that you sent me and loved them even as you loved me (John 17:20, 21, 23).

The great gift of longing, which leads to fulfillment in companionship with Christ, is depicted for us in the first passage of the Song.

The Song (1:2–4)

(She)

> 2 *Let him kiss me with the kisses of his mouth! For your love is better than wine;*
>
> 3 *your anointing oils are fragrant; your name is oil poured out; therefore virgins love you.*
>
> 4 *Draw me after you; let us run. The king has brought me into his chambers.*

(Chorus)

> 4c *We will exult and rejoice in you; we will extol your love more than wine;*

(She)

> 4d *rightly do they love you.*

The Bride's Appraisal of Her Husband

"Let him kiss me with the kisses of his mouth!"

Already, we may be wondering how on earth to understand this Christologically! We will get to that in due time. Let's just consider the story first. This thing begins with a flame. She wants to be kissed—not a peck on the cheek or a kiss of greeting like we read about in the New Testament.[4] No, she says in the next line, "For your love is better than wine" (1:2). She longs for passionate, romantic kisses. Her

---

[4] Rom. 16:16; 1 Cor. 16:20; 2 Cor. 13:12; 1 Thess. 5:26; 1 Pet. 5:14

comment indicates that she knows from experience the quality of his romantic love and she wants more of it.[5]

Yet, we would be wrong to think that she is only interested in one thing—physical consummation. She does want physical consummation, but she wants it because of his whole person. She finds him immensely desirable and enjoyable, not simply because of his physical characteristics, but because of his person, as we find in the following lines.

"Your anointing oils are fragrant; your name is oil poured out" (1:3a). We like things that smell good. The perfume and cologne industries exist because the right smell is very attractive. However, there is something even more compelling to her than his physical aroma—he smells good, but his *name* is more fragrant. His name is oil poured out.

In the Bible, a person's name represented his or her purpose or character.[6] Who he is as a person is overwhelmingly attractive to her. It's more powerful than the alluring fragrance of his body. In fact, it seems from the rest of the Song that his character is the main attraction for her. She does praise him physically in chapter 5, but his character and the way he loves her is what draws her in, intoxicating her.

"Therefore virgins love you," she says (1:3b). He is objectively desirable. She is not the only one who sees it. This may seem like a strange thing to say to one's mate, but it will be very important later.

"Draw me after you; let us run" (1:4a). "Whisk me away!" This woman is not like the aggressive women of our culture, who want to be in the driver's seat. She's also not completely passive, like many other women. She is beautifully right in the middle.[7] She is not going to drive, but she desires him. A modern paraphrase of her message

---

[5] This is one of many comments in the Song that leads me to believe that the man and woman are married from the outset. Not only does this comment indicate that she has already experienced his love, but it would be highly inappropriate for a single woman to speak this way.

[6] Examples: Jacob—Gen. 25:26, cf 27:36, 32:28; Moses—Exo. 2:10; Nabal—1 Sam. 25:25; Jesus—Matt. 1:21

[7] O'Donnell, *The Song of Solomon: An Invitation to Intimacy*, 31. Iain M. Duguid, *Song of Songs*, Reformed Expository Commentary (Phillipsburg, New Jersey: P&R Publishing, 2016), 7.

might be, "Hey, this car of love—drive this thing. I want to go somewhere! Sweep me off my feet. And please hurry!"

"The king has brought me into his chambers" (1:4b).[8] Because she calls him "the king," some have concluded this must be Solomon. I already made the case in the previous chapter why I do not think that is the case. Later, she will describe him as a shepherd. Solomon was not a shepherd. Maybe the man is a literal king, but based upon the rest of the Song, it is more likely that he is a literal shepherd and a figurative king. He is *her* king. His love is juxtaposed with that of the literal King Solomon, who serves as a foil in the Song. Solomon, a literal king, spreads himself among a great many women. However, in the eyes and heart of the woman of the Song, her husband is king, and hers alone. Her king has brought her into his chambers. He has made her his. She wants to be swept off her feet; he has obliged. The desire that she has for him is fulfilled.

Then the female chorus echoes her appraisal of him with what sounds like worship: "We will exult and rejoice in you; we will extol your love more than wine…" (1:4c).[9] This validates what the woman said in verse 3, "therefore virgins love you." His love is praiseworthy. This is widely recognized.

The last line of verse 4 is uttered by the woman: "Rightly do they love you" (1:4d). She's talking about the chorus. "They love you and they are right to do so. You are wonderful." He is uniquely and obviously desirable.

Christ, Our Longing

The Lord Jesus is intended to be the object of our greatest longing, and we are intended to be *constantly fulfilled* in Him. Jesus said, "Whoever comes to me shall not hunger, and whoever believes in me shall never thirst" (John 6:35). He is to be enjoyed in all his fullness by His bride. "Let him kiss me with the kisses of his mouth; For your

---

[8] Here is another reference that makes it difficult to claim they are not already married.

[9] This chorus, elsewhere referred to as the daughters of Jerusalem, play an important role in the Song, and Solomon uses them to convey important things and move the Song along. We need to remember that this is just that—a song. We may be tempted to ask questions like, why is this group of women having a conversation with a husband and wife? It's just a song. Follow the text where it goes without trying to get behind it.

love is better than wine" speaks of both experiential satisfaction and ongoing longing (1:2). We are meant to know the satisfying pleasure of Christ's presence and to want it all the more. The Holy Spirit inspired sexual metaphors to depict spiritual pleasure in Christ because sexual pleasure is a sensation with which we can identify. Christ is the highest of pleasures.

For many in the church, desiring Jesus is an altogether elusive passion. We want to want Him, but we don't. Why? Like the husband in the Song, Jesus is desirable because of His great love and His sterling character. If we don't desire Him, it must be because these things are far removed from our thoughts and daily experience. If we would long for Him and be fulfilled, we must be enamored with His character, love, and work.

It's commonly the case that our hearts burned brightly for Him in the days and months after conversion. Yet, there was a cooling of our affections that left us wondering if He had gone away in some sense. As a pastor, I have witnessed this often.

The Lord's words to the Ephesian church in Revelation 2 may give both the reason for this cooling and the best remedy: "...you have abandoned the love you had at first. Remember therefore from where you have fallen; repent, and do the works you did at first" (Rev. 2:4–5). In those seasons of waning affection for Jesus, it may be that we, not the Lord, have withdrawn. We stopped reading about Him, meditating on His cross and love, talking about Him to others, and seeking Him in prayer. The solution? "Do the works you did at first." Very simply, we must encounter Him in the Scriptures and meditate on His excellencies.

This is not such a foreign concept when we think of it in a different context. My wife and I met on July 12, 1994. We celebrate it every year. Most years on that anniversary, we talk through the events of that day and the following week. We've done it so many times, yet it never gets old. Sometimes when I'm having trouble sleeping, I'll rehearse those days in my own mind. Seeing her for the first time. The first conversation. The first movie. The first hug. It's like pouring fuel on the fire. I love this woman!

The Bible is full of material for just this sort of reminiscing about the Lord. We can go to any number of passages in the Scriptures to

meditate on the character, love, and work of Jesus. As mentioned in
the last chapter, Jesus read the entire Old Testament as something like
a pre-biography about Himself. If we learn to read the Old Testament
as the New Testament authors did, we will never run out of material
for meditation unto greater affection for Him.[10]

In addition to reading and meditating on Christ-centered passages
in the Old Testament, we can read the Gospels, looking for and
dwelling on the character of Christ displayed there. The Gospels are
full of windows into the heart of Christ, prompting us to awe and
wonder, calling us to consider, "Where have I seen Him work this way
in me?" The calming of the storm when He was in the boat with the
disciples—when has the Lord's presence been *my* shelter in stormy
trials? The healing of a leper—how has Christ compassionately
touched my sin-diseased heart? The raising of Lazarus from the
dead—where and what was I when He called *me* from death to life?
Most of us who have known the Lord for long have numerous

---

[10] Some great go-to passages would include:

Isa. 53:3, "He was despised and rejected by men; a man of sorrows, and acquainted
with grief; and as one from whom men hide their faces he was despised, and we
esteemed him not."

Psa. 16:10, "For you will not abandon my soul to Sheol, or let your holy one see
corruption."

Psa. 22:1, "My God, my God, why have you forsaken me? Why are you so far from
saving me, from the words of my groaning?"

Song 8:6, "Set me as a seal upon your heart, as a seal upon your arm, for love is strong
as death, jealousy is fierce as the grave. Its flashes are flashes of fire, the very flame of
the LORD."

Acts 2:23–24, "...this Jesus, delivered up according to the definite plan and
foreknowledge of God, you crucified and killed by the hands of lawless men. God
raised him up, loosing the pangs of death, because it was not possible for him to be
held by it."

Rom. 5:1, "Therefore, since we have been justified by faith, we have peace with God
through our Lord Jesus Christ."

1 Cor. 15:22, "For as in Adam all die, so also in Christ shall all be made alive."

Eph. 2:6, "[God] raised us up with him and seated us with him in the heavenly
places..."

Phil. 2:8, "And being found in human form, he humbled himself by becoming
obedient to the point of death, even death on a cross."

Tit. 3:4–5a, "But when the goodness and loving kindness of God our Savior appeared,
he saved us, not because of works done by us in righteousness, but according to his
own mercy."

(Very shortly, the entire Song of Songs will read to us like a testament to the character
and love of Jesus, a wonderful place for meditation.)

instances we can recall when the Jesus of the Gospels manifested Himself in personal ways. We should return to these things often and cherish Him.

Perhaps the greatest way to fan into flame our passion for Jesus is to daily rehearse the story of the gospel itself, using rich teaching from both Testaments for fuel. I've used the following statements for this purpose for years:

God is holy. This holy Creator made all people, including me, for the glorious purpose of knowing Him and bearing His image. (Lev. 10; Isa. 6:3; Psa. 99:9)

Man is sinful. The first man rebelled against God's plan, as did I. I've sinned against Him too many times and in too many ways to count. My heart itself was a breeding ground of sin. (Gen. 3; Rom. 3:10–18, 23)

God is wrathful. God is a just judge. He brings righteous justice upon every sin ever committed, including every sin I've ever committed. Every heinous act; every ungodly attitude. (John 3:36; Rom. 3:23; Eph. 2:1–3)

Man is doomed. There is nothing I could do to escape God's judgment in hell. I was trapped in sin, helpless to change myself or to atone for my wrongdoing. (Matt. 3:12, 7:13, 8:12, 10:28, 13:38–42; Rom. 3:10–20; 2 Thess. 1:9)

God is gracious. The heart of God is kind to sinners. He moved to rescue me from my self-inflicted agony. (Exo. 34:6; Eph. 2:4–7)

Christ was given. The righteous life that I could never live, God the Son lived in my stead. The death that I deserved, the Lord of Glory died for me on the cross. My sins He bore in His body on the tree that I might die to sin and live to righteousness. (John 3:16; 2 Cor. 5:21; 1 Pet. 2:24–25; 1 John 4:10)

God was satisfied. Jesus' righteous life and atoning death were pleasing to God, as demonstrated by the resurrection on the third day. Jesus satisfied God's wrath on my behalf and earned the right to give me life eternal. (Acts 2:24–36; 1 Cor. 15:12–23; 1 Pet. 1:3–5)

Man is redeemed. Through repentance and faith, I was reconciled to God, adopted into His family, and made joint heirs with the Lord Jesus of all the blessings in the heavenly places. My beloved is mine and I am His. (Song 2:16; Matt. 3:2; John 3:16; Acts 2:38–39; 3:19–21; 17:30–31; Rom. 3:23–25; Eph. 2:8)

The gospel should be on our minds daily. To the extent that it is, we will love it and love Him.

All of this is not mere theological navel-gazing. Longing pulls us to fulfillment. We meditate on His character, love, and work so that we are moved to enjoy fellowship with Him and worship Him. We find this longing in the Song of Songs between the man and the woman. The man's name, his character, the truth about who he is, is not enough for the woman. It draws her to want his kisses, to want his fellowship. "Come here!"

Oh, that we would have hearts toward Christ like this woman toward her husband! What a glorious thing to find ourselves drawn inexorably to worship Him when we read the Word, pray, and interact with other believers. Oh, that we would find it intolerable to miss a worship service, our heart saying, "I have to get in on this. I have to engage with Him. I have to lift my hands and raise my voice to Him."

When we miss Jesus as the ultimate longing of our hearts, we miss everything and open ourselves up to settling for counterfeits. Just as Psalm 16 concludes with the truth that fullness of joy is found in the presence of Christ, it also reveals the outcome of pursuing other gods, "The sorrows of those who run after another god shall multiply" (Psa. 16:4). When our highest longing is someone or something other than the Lord Jesus, the result is not merely the growth of our sorrows, but the multiplication of them. Perhaps this is why many husbands and wives are so miserable in their marriages: they have been looking to one another to provide ultimate meaning and satisfaction when only Christ can provide it.

Have you longed for closeness and intimacy with your spouse with an intensity that you have not longed for fellowship with Christ? If so, you have been running after another god. Is it any wonder your sorrows have multiplied?[11]

---

[11] In the Old Testament, the prophets made much of the silliness of idol worship. The people would take one tree and use part of it as fuel to cook their food. Taking the rest, they would carve an idol and pray to it (Isa. 44:14–17; cf Hos. 4:12; Jer. 10:5). The people abandoned the One True God in favor of ridiculous substitutes of their own design. In their moment of greatest need, these false gods were useless to help (Deut. 32:37–38; Jer. 2:28). We don't want to take the analogy too far. Your spouse is

When Christ is your ultimate longing, you will never fail to be satisfied, nor will you be completely devastated when lesser pleasures fail you. Even if your spouse ends up being nothing like you hoped, as long as Christ is your highest longing and satisfaction, sorrow cannot overtake you. You will know "pleasures forevermore" at the right hand of God where Christ is (Psa. 16:11)! Make Christ the object of your greatest longing. You will know ultimate fulfillment in Him, *and* you will be equipped to know the lesser joy of a fulfilling marriage.

Pursuing Godly Character

When we read the Song and behold the woman's intense desire due to her husband's sterling character, we may reflexively think, "Yeah, my spouse isn't like that. My spouse has no desire for me whatsoever." Why might that desire be missing? It may have something to do with the aforementioned sterling character, or more accurately, lack thereof.

Why did our spouses desire us in the beginning? To be perfectly honest, they thought we were someone else. We put our best foot forward, hiding our faults, perhaps even pretending to have a certain caliber of character, until we were married and could no longer keep up the pretense. Our hearts betrayed us in the day-to-day activities of married life. Eventually, our spouses learned who we really are, and it served to cool what was once a bright red flame.

The woman of the Song desires her husband for two reasons. His love is better than wine, and his name is oil poured out. That is, he loves well, and he has impeccable character (recall that biblical names often depict the character of the person). We might assume those two things are unrelated, but they are not. The former flows from the latter.

My daughter recently played Ariel in a theatrical adaptation of *The Little Mermaid*. If we put aside the terrible messages the story teaches about teens knowing better than their parents, there are helpful lessons. One is that character trumps appearance and abilities. Ursula

---

a gift from God, which we will consider shortly. But when it comes to the capacity for providing ultimate fulfillment, your spouse is as ill-equipped to satisfy as a piece of firewood is to save a nation from foreign invaders. Only Christ can give that for which you long.

the Sea Witch takes Ariel's voice and transforms herself from a tentacled beast into a beautiful woman so that she looks and sounds like a brunette Ariel. Pretty face, pretty voice—why not marry her, Eric?

Suppose we do a "choose-your-own-adventure" with the end of the story. Let's say Eric does marry the incognito Ursula. And let's say she never turns back into a huge octopus-woman. Will they live happily ever after? No! She still has the heart of a dragon and wants to rule the universe. Eventually, that side of her will come out. Can you imagine Eric saying, "Yes, she's pure evil and mean as a snake, but her love is better than wine"? I can't see that. She would be as desirable to Eric as the forbidden woman of Proverbs 5:4: "In the end, she is bitter as wormwood, sharp as a two-edged sword."

Remove the high character of the husband of the Song and the woman would never have said, "Your love is better than wine," nor "Let him kiss me with the kisses of his mouth" (1:2). She finds him desirable; she wants his love precisely because of who he is.

Of course, this concept is exemplified in Christ. He is ultimately desirable because of His infinite perfections. The better we know His excellencies, the more we find fellowship with Him pleasurable. If we would emulate how Christ exemplifies the love of this section of the Song, we must pursue Christlike character with a holy passion so as to create an atmosphere of fulfillment for our spouses. As we grow in godliness, we are better able to love as Christ does, creating a place where it is quite easy for our spouses to reflect the beauty of the gospel with us.

Remember that we must not seek *ultimate* fulfillment in marriage. That comes only through Christ. Yet, because marriage is intended to be a picture of the relationship between Christ and the church, it must be fulfilling. To that end, your pursuit of godly character is essential to your spouse's fulfillment because only as you grow in Christlikeness will you love as He loves.

Putting Off and Putting On

Growth in godly character involves using the means of fellowship with Christ—addressed more fully in a later chapter—in conjunction with a biblical concept that some have called "putting off and putting on." The Bible rarely tells us to jettison a sinful action or attitude without commanding a corresponding godly action or attitude to take its place. The typical approach of the biblical authors is to say, "Get rid of this AND put this in its place."

The principle is stated quite clearly in Colossians 3:9–10: "…You have put off the old self with its practices and have put on the new self, which is being renewed in knowledge after the image of its creator." In usual Pauline fashion, the apostle calls us to live in accordance with what has been accomplished for us in Christ. When we repented and trusted in Jesus, we turned away from our old sinful way of life and turned toward a life of faith in Him. Growth in godliness entails the repeated decision to live in light of our new life. We do this moment-by-moment by turning away from the ungodliness typical of our former spiritual death, and by trusting in the power of Christ to help us walk in the godliness typical of our resurrection life.

I have an old, long-sleeve t-shirt from my alma mater that my wife has been wishing into the trash heap for years now. It has so many holes that it would be indecent to wear without another t-shirt underneath. The cuffs are held on by a couple of threads and positive thinking. The school logo on the front is little more than a rumor. I love it. I can do anything in that shirt: work in the garage, climb up in the attic, decompose, etc. Any dirty job is perfectly appropriate for it. I have another shirt that is on the other end of the spectrum. It has one purpose—staying clean. It fits well, looks nice. My wife loves it. I would never dream of doing anything in it other than preaching or going on a date.

There are certain activities appropriate to the first shirt that are not appropriate to the second—unthinkable, actually. I would never wear my dress shirt to clean out the gutters or mow the lawn. The opposite is true, as well. I would never wear the old ratty shirt…well, to do anything around other humans.

When we were saved, it was like we exchanged garments with Christ. We wore horribly soiled clothes, tainted by sin. Jesus wore gleaming white clothes indicative of perfect righteousness. At the cross, we traded. He took the penalty deserved by our filthiness, and now we enjoy the blessings deserved by His purity. We wear the righteousness of Christ and, on that basis, we are declared righteous by the Father.

Yet, because we are not perfectly sanctified in our character and conduct, we tend to behave like people still wearing filthy clothes. As we seek to grow in godliness, we must regularly think in terms of what is befitting the righteousness of Christ that we wear like a garment. In what ways am I living like I am wearing those old sinful rags? I must prayerfully put them off and put on the character and conduct consistent with the righteousness of Jesus.

In my experience, few believers have any idea what attitudes and actions are most needful of replacing with Christlike alternatives. For the love of Christ and spouse, we should each regularly take stock of where we tend to revert to the "old self," and do those things necessary to grow toward godliness in those precise areas. It requires great intentionality.

Our pursuit of godliness, ultimately a reflection of our affection for Christ, is secondarily a gift to our spouse. We do not give in order to get, as is the mentality of so many marriage self-helps out there. We do not seek to grow in godliness so that our spouse will desire us and then give us what we want. Rather, this is all about giving. We need a Christlike "give in order to give" mentality. In the next chapter, we will consider the other side of this coin—loving our spouses in spite of their imperfections. So, we are not advocating earning one another's love. We are advocating pursuing a Christlike character that creates longing for intimacy, a great blessing to our spouse.

Jesus At the Center

I hope you are beginning to see how essential Jesus is to this pursuit of a godly marriage. If we take the Song of Songs and treat it like a typical self-help marriage book, finding some practical applications and determining what we can do better on a relational level, we will have failed miserably. We cannot miss Christ in this Song. Passion for Jesus is the motive and power to do what needs to be done in our marriages. If you jump over the Christological elements, if you don't find Jesus more appealing, if you don't find your heart echoing the woman, saying of Jesus, "Call me after you; let us run," if passionate fellowship with Jesus does not eventuate from your time in this Song, applying it to your marriage is a lost cause. It will not work.

Discussion Questions/Activities

1. What is the highest longing of your life? The following clues may lead you there: How do you spend your discretionary time? When you don't have to think about anything else, where do your thoughts go?

2. What value is there in meditating on the Lord's character? Rehearsing His saving acts? How can you incorporate these things into your daily life?

3. Sit down with your spouse and discuss the ways in which you both are reverting to the "old self." First, confess your observations of your own failures to your spouse. Second, invite your spouse to comment on those failures and help you see other glaring instances you may have missed. Third, switch places and repeat steps one and two.

4. What are the biblical names for the failures identified in #3? What we may call "moodiness" may more accurately be called by the biblical phrase "sinful anger." What we refer to as "insensitive comments," the Bible may call "slander."

5. What are the biblical attributes that you need to "put on" for every sinful attribute you need to "put off" in #4? What biblical passages can you find about both the sinful attributes and godly attributes?

6. Memorize one Scripture verse for your most needful "put off" and "put on."

04

BELONGING

No Place Like Home

I have a love/hate relationship with cheesy movie lines and song lyrics. They make me nauseous, yet they're so intriguing as an insight into the deep longings of the human heart. Admittedly, songwriters and screenwriters are in a bind. Themes common to the human experience must be their subject matter in order for the audience to relate. At the same time, no one wants to hear it done the same way over and over. There are only so many ways to say, "I love you," and "How could you do this to me?" So, these creative types are left to do their dead-level best to re-plow old ground day after day. I should give them a break, I guess. It must be terrible.

One such theme that has found both heartwarming and clumsy expression is the desire to find a place of belonging. Of course, there is the classic cheese-laden Tom Cruise line from *Jerry Maguire*—so bad that other movies make fun of it: "You...complete...me." Its less clunky echo can be heard in *The Mirror Has Two Faces*, as Jeff Bridges says to Barbra Streisand: "When I'm with you, I feel as if...well, as if I'm home."

Then there is the not at all corny, but ridiculously catchy theme song to the 80's sitcom, *Cheers*:

Sometimes you want to go
Where everybody knows your name
And they're always glad you came
You want to be where you can see
Our troubles are all the same
You want to be where everybody knows your name

Anyway, you get the idea. This theme keeps finding its way into movies and songs because everyone longs to belong. It's the feeling of every kid who doesn't want to be the last one picked when choosing teams. It's in the heart of every girl waiting to be asked to the prom. It's the desire of military children who want desperately not to be the new kids all the time. Toddlers, children, teens, adults, and seniors of all cultures know exactly what this is like. Everyone wants to belong.

We could say it's a desire that originated when Adam and Eve were cast out of the garden. They had the perfect place of fulfillment and belonging but lost it when they sinned against God and were removed from His presence. The story of Old Testament Israel is a kind of search for a place to belong—safety and fellowship with God. Abraham, called to be a nomad, was promised that he would be the father of a multitude and that his descendants would enjoy a special place of covenantal fellowship with God.[1] They did come into the land of promise, yet, like Adam and Eve, they were unable to hold onto this paradise because of their unfaithfulness to God. As long as a place of belonging depends upon human performance, man will only be disappointed.

We have become heirs of desires that can only be fulfilled in Christ. By His life, death, and resurrection, He creates the place of belonging where our performance is not the basis of our inclusion. It's a place of tremendous safety and joy. The Song of Songs strikes this theme from its very outset.

The Song (1:5–8)
(She)
5 I am very dark, but lovely, O daughters of Jerusalem, like the
tents of Kedar, like the curtains of Solomon.

---

[1] Gen. 12:1–3, 15:1–21

6 Do not gaze at me because I am dark, because the sun has looked upon me. My mother's sons were angry with me; they made me keeper of the vineyards, but my own vineyard I have not kept!
7 Tell me, you whom my soul loves, where you pasture your flock, where you make it lie down at noon; for why should I be like one who veils herself beside the flocks of your companions?

(He)
8 If you do not know, O most beautiful among women, follow in the tracks of the flock, and pasture your young goats beside the shepherds' tents.

The Bride's Appraisal of Herself

"I am very dark, but lovely, O daughters of Jerusalem, like the tents of Kedar, like the curtains of Solomon. Do not gaze at me because I am dark, because the sun has looked upon me. My mother's sons were angry with me; they made me keeper of the vineyards, but my own vineyard I have not kept!" (1:5–6). What a contrast she draws between her husband and herself! He is ultimately desirable and young women praise him. On the other hand, she is not ultimately desirable. She is unattractive and reports a group of young men who were upset with her. He's top tier; she's bottom shelf.

"The sun has looked upon me," she says (1:6). She is deeply tanned. We find a good tan highly attractive in our culture, going to great lengths to acquire one. Some of us find it more elusive than others. (People like me have two shades—lily white and trip-to-the-burn-unit.) Tan is attractive to us. However, in the ancient Near East, a tan meant you were low-class. You worked outside. Nobody wanted a tan back then. They wanted to be light-skinned. Still, the woman says she's lovely. It's possible that she means she's pretty, but you wouldn't know it because she's too dark; she's been damaged by the sun. By the standards of the culture, she's unattractive.

"Do not gaze at me because I am dark," she says to the daughters of Jerusalem, self-conscious about her appearance (1:6). The text is a bit vague, but there is a backstory regarding her family. Her "mother's sons," her brothers, were angry at her and made her work outside as a keeper of the vineyards. "But my own vineyard I have not kept," she says, using the word "vineyard" with two different meanings (1:6). Her brothers made her a keeper of literal vineyards, but she has not kept her own vineyard in a figurative sense, referring to her own appearance. Because of the work imposed on her, she has not been able to give attention to her body. Her appearance has suffered because of her need to focus on hard work.

If we compare these verses to those we considered in the last chapter, we see that she is a contrast to him. She is not attractive. No one recognizes her beauty. Others were angry with her rather than singing her praises. She has not been able to give attention to her vineyard, to her appearance. She's not like him.

Considering his perfection and her reasonable self-consciousness, one would expect her to shy away from him, to think that he is obviously out of her league. For this reason, her disposition toward him is surprising:

"Tell me, you whom my soul loves, where you pasture your flock, where you make it lie down at noon; for why should I be like one who veils herself beside the flocks of your companions?" (1:7). Again, she is culturally undesirable and very self-conscious...but drawn to him. She wants to be with him. She describes him as a shepherd, a protector. She feels safe with him. Perhaps, this explains her comment regarding the veil. With others, she must cover her face. With him, she is free to be open and unashamed.

In a somewhat playful response, he replies in verse 8, "If you do not know, O most beautiful among women, follow in the tracks of the flock, and pasture your young goats beside the shepherds' tents." Not only does he tell her where to go, but in light of what she has revealed about herself he calls her by a most outrageous name: O most beautiful among women. No wonder she wants to be with him! No wonder she feels safe and accepted by him—he doesn't see her the way others do. He doesn't see her the way she sees herself. To him she is the most beautiful of all. We might say, she is objectively unattractive, but in his eyes, she is the most beautiful among women.

Despite her imperfections, she feels safe with him. Remember that poetry is not intended primarily to impart information, but to impart longing. For what are we intended to long in these verses? We are intended to long for the kind of love depicted: a love where a person feels safe and wanted in spite of imperfections. It is a place of belonging.

Christ, Our Place of Belonging

Like the shepherdess of the Song, we were damaged, unattractive, and imperfect. We had nothing to commend us to the Savior. Paul describes our natural state in Romans 1:29–31:

> They were filled with all manner of unrighteousness, evil, covetousness, malice. They are full of envy, murder, strife, deceit, maliciousness. They are gossips, slanderers, haters of God, insolent, haughty, boastful, inventors of evil, disobedient to parents, foolish, faithless, heartless, ruthless.

"Guilty, vile, and helpless we," as the hymn writer put it.[2] Damaged and unattractive, to say the least. The shepherdess of the Song has much more to commend her than we did—she loves her shepherd king. From our conception, our hearts beat to rebel against God. We are natural-born Christ-haters.

But graciously, the King has brought us into His chamber through His death on the cross and His resurrection on the third day. He is a shepherd who cares for us, protects us, and loves us as if we are unblemished. At the point of our conversion, when we repent and trust in His atoning death on the cross, our character is not instantly changed. We all know this experientially. We continue to struggle with sin. "We all stumble in many ways" (Jas. 3:2). Yet, His love and acceptance are not based upon what He finds in us, but upon what He has given to us: His righteousness credited to our account.[3] That unconditional love allows us to draw near to Christ with confidence, wearing His righteousness even as we know that in our own character and conduct we are riddled with imperfections. His unconditional love says to us, in a sense, "You're safe with Me. You're safe in Me. And because of what I've done, you're beautiful." If we know Christ truly,

---

[2] From "Hallelujah! What a Savior!" by Philip P. Bliss, published in 1875.
[3] Rom. 5:17–19

we will feel loved and accepted by Him in spite of our imperfections. He has brought us into His chamber. He is our place of belonging.

This phenomenon is unique to Jesus' love for us. Our educational system, our economy, our athletics, even the world of romance is based upon competition. You get out of it what you put into it. We are so wired to live within the framework of a performance mentality that the gospel can seem too good to be true. Many believers profess to believe yet live as if their standing with God still depends upon their own merit. Some believers suffer from what has been called "morbid introspection," a tendency to constantly look inward, wondering how their performance is affecting God's disposition toward them. They are forever evaluating their own motives, parsing their words, weighing their sins against their godly fruit, calculating the score.

We must keep in mind that God has designed the gospel to graciously give us a place of belonging while depriving us of any place of boasting. Ephesians 2:8–9 explains just how essential grace is to the great plan of God: "For by grace you have been saved through faith. And this is not your own doing; it is the gift of God, not a result of works, so that no one may boast." By this, God glorifies Himself, showing "the immeasurable riches of his grace in kindness toward us in Christ Jesus" (Eph. 2:7).

When we approach the Lord with a performance-based mentality, we make two horrible mistakes. First, we misunderstand the gospel after claiming to believe it. That is, we think our works, not Christ's, make us right with the Father. This effectively takes our eyes off the Lord Jesus and places them back upon ourselves. Second and related, we denigrate Jesus by implying that His righteous life and atoning death were not sufficient to secure a right standing with God. Given these two possible mistakes, we must ask ourselves: Is it that we do not really believe the gospel? Or, is it simply that we cannot stand for Jesus to receive all the glory? Whichever is the case, we should repent and become enamored with this Savior who gave all of Himself so that our deplorable offenses would be overwhelmed by His righteousness in the final accounting.

This is not to say that we should have no awareness of our lingering sin. Certainly, the more we love Him, the more we will hate sin. Yet, like the bride in the Song, our imperfection will not cause us to hide from Him, but His love will draw us ever closer despite that imperfection.

Further, His great love becomes our greatest weapon in the ongoing fight against sin. Meditation upon His unconditional love is what moves us to desire fellowship with Him. He is truly the only person who loves us without reference to our performance. This inexplicable affection flowing from Him causes our affection for Him to grow, which ironically increases our desire to live in ways that please Him. While we do not draw His love upon us by our performance, His love moves us to want to perform for His pleasure!

At our church we sing a wonderful song which contains the lines, "Take His easy yoke and wear it / Love will make your obedience sweet…Blessed are the eyes that see Him / Blessed the ears that hear His voice…His commandments then become their happy choice."[4] So loving is this Savior and so compelling is His presence that we are willingly transformed in our character and conduct.

Something beautiful will happen in this Song as we continue to read. At the beginning, the woman's imperfections are highlighted. However, as her husband loves her, she is transformed and is eventually described with the same terms he is. In other words, his love makes her like him. That's what Christ does for us. As we think about these things, we should be moved to be close to him. And we should want to be like him in these things. A glorious forum for that is in our marriages.

Unconditional Love

In the last chapter, we considered emulating Christ by pursuing His sterling character to create an atmosphere of fulfillment for our spouses. Now, we will look at the other side of that coin: loving our spouses in spite of their imperfections.

Perhaps your desire for your spouse is all but dead because of the character he/she has exhibited over the years. You may remember a better time earlier in your marriage, but even your reflection on that time is somewhat cynical. I have heard it expressed this way: "Well, yes, I desired my spouse like that when we were newlyweds, or before

---

[4] "Come, Ye Souls by Sin Afflicted." Words: Joseph Swain; Music: Kevin Twit; ©2013 Kevin Twit Music (ASCAP)

we married, but then I got to know my spouse. They say familiarity breeds contempt. That's just the natural life cycle of a marriage. At first, you think your spouse is wonderful. He/she doesn't have faults, and for that reason, you're powerfully drawn to him/her. Then as you get to know all your spouse's imperfections, the desire cools to a certain extent. This is just normal. You can't expect people who have been married for years and years to desire one another like newlyweds do. They know each other too well."

Have you ever heard that or said it yourself? Let's walk through this a little bit. If the above quote even resembles your thoughts, it means that you have grown *comfortable* not desiring your spouse because of your spouse's imperfections. You've embraced that as normal. However, as we read the Song, we find that this woman has obvious imperfections and yet she feels safe and desired by this man. Her husband loves her, accepts her, desires her in spite of her imperfections, which is what Jesus does for us. Being okay with a "normal" where we don't desire our spouse because of the spouse's imperfections is not like Jesus. It instead resembles the world.

Our culture gives lip service to accepting people just the way they are but does not practice what it preaches. It is the spirit of this fallen age to love and accept people for what they offer us. How common is it to see two people desiring one another only to the extent that their spouses have earned it? It is the spirit of the world to say, "I don't desire you because you're imperfect."

Jesus is nothing like that. He loves us without reference to our imperfections. The Bible calls us to be Jesus to our spouses, to pursue our spouses in spite of their imperfections, just like Jesus does with us.

A husband and wife desiring each other without reference to their mutual imperfections is a dynamite picture of the gospel. It is one reason why we must keep the gospel in front of ourselves all the time, reminding ourselves that we are loved despite our performance. We were saved despite our imperfections. This knowledge causes our affection for Christ to grow, and as our affection for Christ grows, our hearts say, "I want to be like him." A most obvious arena in which we should be like Him is in our marriages.

Gospel-believing people should have gospel-resembling marriages. Our marriages should be the safest places on earth in terms of love and acceptance. And yet in many Christian marriages, that is not the case. I am aware of Christian marriages where spouses are constantly criticizing one another, calling one another names, tearing one another down. Regrettably, I have found it quite common in my ministry for believing husbands and wives to compare each other, out loud and unfavorably, to other men and women. For example, a husband will make comments about how desirable another woman's body is compared to his wife's body. I have heard wives do the same thing. It happens not just with reference to the other's body, but their character, as well. Such a state of affairs screams, "Perfection is the cost of my love. I say I believe the gospel, but I feel no obligation to live it!" What kind of atmosphere does that create in a marriage? Not one of safety, delightful vulnerability, and open sharing. If imitation of Christ is our calling, this is sacrilege. A godly marriage is one where both spouses are safe in their imperfections.

Some people are very quick to say, "We are not capable of unconditional love." Consider the "Love Command" of John 13:34, "A new commandment I give to you, that you love one another: just as I have loved you, you also are to love one another." If this is a command to all believers to love one another as Christ does—in a sense, to be Christ to one another—how much more should it apply to two believers joined in marriage? As Jesus spoke to His disciples in John 13, He knew that He was going away and was speaking a word of comfort to them. "I'm going away, but don't worry—I'll still love and care for you…through one another." As Jesus gave that command to love as He loves, He did so with a straight face. Should we really understand His command to contain an implicit caveat? "Love one another as I have loved you…except of course for that whole unconditional part. Obviously, you're not capable of that." Perish the thought!

If you have ever thought, "Oh, I can't love like Jesus loved," His words recorded just a few verses later are for you: "Truly, truly, I say to you, whoever believes in me will also do the works that I do; and greater works than these will he do, because I am going to the Father" (John 14:12). Later in the same passage, Jesus promised the gifts of powerful prayer and of the indwelling Holy Spirit, both intended to empower us to do just what Jesus commanded in John 13:34—to love as He has loved us. He not only commands it, but He gives us the ability to do it. The idea that a believer—bought by the blood of Christ to live for Christ, inhabited by the very Spirit of Christ, and invited by Christ to pray outrageous prayers and expect affirmative answers—cannot love unconditionally is not only a cop-out, but it is untrue!

Additionally, you've almost certainly already promised to do it. Anyone who had anything like traditional vows at their wedding ceremony made a promise to love unconditionally. I am not aware of any Christian wedding vows that say anything like, "I promise to love you as long as you stay on my good side, or as long as your character is what I perceive it to be today, or as long as you're kind to me, or as long as you're perfect, or as long as you don't hurt me." What a Christless set of vows those would be!

What do the vows say? "Till death do us part." Perhaps we should say there is one condition: your spouse must be breathing for you to be obligated to continue to love them.[5] But that is the one condition. It is not all the other conditions that we tend to tack on after the fact.

There is a certain sense of freedom that comes from making the decision, "I'm going to love my spouse regardless of what he/she does or proves to be." The determination to love your spouse regardless of his/her performance, to be a place of belonging with all his/her imperfections will always enjoy the glowing approval of the Christ who inspired it. It will fortify your dependence upon and enjoyment of Jesus Himself. Why? First, He is the one who will enable you to do it. Second, being Christlike is *pleasurable*. How overlooked this is! Jesus found it pleasurable to love the unlovely because He is perfect in love, joy, peace, patience, kindness, goodness, faithfulness, gentleness, and self-control. These just happen to be the attributes His Spirit works in those who belong to Him.

To the person who still fears, "Whether I change or not, my spouse will continue to love me based upon my performance": be encouraged—you are in good company. Jesus knows exactly what it is like to love others who either love Him not at all or love Him poorly.

---

[5] Rom. 7:2; 1 Cor. 7:39

He has gone before you in this, doing exactly what seems impossible to you now. He has loved the unlovely regardless of what He gets in return. And graciously, He offers you help: "For we do not have a high priest who is unable to sympathize with our weaknesses, but one who in every respect has been tempted as we are, yet without sin. Let us then with confidence draw near to the throne of grace, that we may receive mercy and find grace to help in time of need" (Heb. 4:15–16).

You may recognize you have failed to be Christ to your spouse. The atmosphere of acceptance and love that you enjoy in His presence you have denied to your spouse. Why not confess that to the Lord and to your spouse? Seek forgiveness from both. Wear out your knees praying for change as you pursue meaningful conversations about the issue. Ask your spouse, "What can I do to make you feel safe? Loved?"

May we long for Him and enjoy the belonging that He has created for us with His mighty, unconditional love. And may that move us to make our marriages places of belonging, where we pursue all levels of intimacy with our spouses without reference to what anyone deserves, where our spouses can know they are loved regardless of their performance.

Discussion Questions/Activities

1. How are you like the woman in this section of the Song? How is Christ like the husband?

2. How is it possible for believers to still struggle with sin and yet have a right relationship with the Father?

3. If we continue to approach the Father based upon our performance, what does it indicate about what we believe?

4. How can we fight sin as believers without adopting a performance mentality?

5. Discuss with your spouse the ways your marriage is a place of belonging: how do you both feel accepted despite failures/imperfections? In what specific ways is that missing? If necessary, express repentance to one another and ask for forgiveness.

05

SACHET

An Albatross Around Your Neck

In Samuel Taylor Coleridge's *The Rime of the Ancient Mariner* (1798), the mariner shoots an albatross that has been following his ship. His rash action brings a curse that leads to a tumultuous voyage and the eventual death of all the other sailors. To punish him, his shipmates hang the dead bird around his neck to be his only companion as he is forced to watch fate's unfolding. Thus, "an albatross around your neck" has come to be a metaphor for something that is burdensome and hinders progress or causes great problems.[1]

Ignorance of the literal albatross takes some of the significance out of both the mariner poem and the metaphor. An albatross is an enormous bird with a wingspan of up to 11 feet. Its wings are so massive that it can glide for hours without flapping them.[2] The mariner wasn't wearing a dead sea parakeet around his neck. It was a massive, foul-smelling burden—a constant reminder of a terrible decision.

---

[1] *Farlex Dictionary of Idioms.* S.v. "albatross around neck." *Collins COBUILD Idioms Dictionary, 3rd ed..* S.v. "albatross around neck." Retrieved March 16 2019 from https://idioms.thefreedictionary.com/albatross+around+neck

[2] *Miriam-Webster Dictionary.* S.v. "albatross." Retrieved March 16 2019 from https://www.merriam-webster.com/dictionary/albatross

In the book of Genesis, God recognized that it was not good for the man to be alone, so He made a helper suitable for the man. Lest we conceive of a helper playing a non-essential supporting role, we should consider how this word is used elsewhere in the Old Testament. The Hebrew word is *ezer* and it is frequently used of God Himself. "Our soul waits for the LORD; he is our *help* and our shield" (Psa. 33:20). "I lift up my eyes to the hills. From where does my help come? My help comes from the LORD, who made heaven and earth" (Psa. 121:1–2).[3] An *ezer* is no superfluous aid, but one who supplies strength and support where it is lacking in the one helped. The man in Genesis 2 was made better because of the woman. She complemented him.

The opposite is true as well in God's design for marriage. The man supplies strength and support in those areas where the woman is lacking. He is what she needs. This is God's ideal Garden of Eden design. Marital love is a great, complementing support to the individual. The love of the one is a metaphorical blessing about the neck of the other.

Surely, this is what so many hope for at the altar. Yet, years or only months later, rather than a blessing about the neck, the husband and wife become more like an albatross. Through their own failure to pursue Christ and their resultant self-seeking, they tempt their spouses to regard them as an emblem of a horrible mistake made by uttering two words: "I do."

But there is good news! God's ideal is not lost to us, not even if we have wasted years making a mess of our marriage. God fixes broken things. The gospel restores us to Eden. We are enabled by the redemption of Christ and the indwelling Spirit to be a blessed benefit to our spouses. The world regularly knows of marriages that start out hot and then cool to indifference at best, war and divorce at worst. Our great Savior exemplifies and enables a better way.

The Song (1:9–14)

(He)

9 I compare you, my love, to a mare among Pharaoh's chariots.

---

[3] Also, Exo. 18:4; Deut. 33:29; Psa. 20:2, 115:9–11, 124:8, 146:5; Hos. 13:9

10 Your cheeks are lovely with ornaments, your neck with strings of jewels.

(Chorus)
11 We will make for you ornaments of gold, studded with silver.

(She)
12 While the king was on his couch, my nard gave forth its fragrance.
13 My beloved is to me a sachet of myrrh that lies between my breasts.
14 My beloved is to me a cluster of henna blossoms in the vineyards of Engedi.

Once again, we notice that the woman is doing most of the talking. The man says and does loving things to and for her, but there are larger sections of her describing his effect on her.

He begins, "I compare you, my love, to a mare among Pharaoh's chariots" (1:9). Many of the compliments in the Song would be off-putting in our culture. Rest assured, he's not exactly saying, "You look like a horse." Ancient sources indicate that Pharaoh's horses were extravagantly decorated. They were magnificent to behold. In verse 10, he interprets himself for us: "Your cheeks are lovely with ornaments, your neck with strings of jewels." She is magnificent to behold.

This is striking given what we know about her. Her skin is damaged by the sun. It's possible she has literal jewelry on her cheeks and neck, but more likely he's using a metaphor. If she has been damaged by the sun, where would that be most obvious? Her cheeks and her neck. Paraphrased, what she thinks is unattractive about herself he finds beautiful: "Your cheeks and neck are gorgeous."

That she is not wearing literal jewelry explains what the chorus says in verse 11: "We will make for you ornaments of gold, studded with silver." They offer to make jewelry for her. This could be taken a couple of ways. They could be celebrating her beauty, or given that she is culturally unattractive, they could be saying, "If jewelry would help, we will be happy to make a bunch of it for you." Their offer will make much more sense once we have come to the end of the passage.

In verse 12, the bride speaks: "While the king was on his couch, my nard gave forth its fragrance." She could be understood to mean, "While the king was loving me, my nard gave forth its fragrance." Nard was used as perfume. However, the coming verses indicate that she is using the word "nard" metaphorically; she is not talking about literal perfume. Rather, she is saying, "While he loved me, I began to smell good." Remember that the Song began with her praising his fragrance. Shortly, as she was giving her appraisal of herself, she said that she had been unable to give such attention to her own body. The contrast was intended to show that he is aesthetically pleasing—looks good, smells good—but that she is not because she has been unable to devote time to those things. But now, as he has loved her, she has begun to smell good. Yet, stay tuned. His aroma and hers are connected as the following verses will show.

Verse 13: "My beloved is to me a sachet of myrrh that lies between my breasts." A sachet is like a leather pouch, and myrrh is another substance known for its pleasing fragrance. What does she say about that pouch of myrrh around her neck? It's him! My beloved is to me a sachet of myrrh… This sachet serves double duty. First, it answers the daughters of Jerusalem. They said essentially, "Let us make jewelry for you to enhance your beauty." With the sachet, she replies, "No, I have a necklace; it's him. He makes me beautiful." Second, the sachet of myrrh is a metaphor for the husband, reinforcing that the earlier aromatic substance—nard—is also a metaphor.

Verse 14 provides a third layer of this fragrance imagery: "My beloved is to me a cluster of henna blossoms in the vineyards of Engedi." The sachet and henna blossoms, both referring to the husband, indicate that the nard, too, is a reference to him— "While the king was on his couch, my nard gave forth its fragrance" (1:12). The fragrant nard, the sachet of myrrh, and the cluster of henna blossoms—all images of alluring aroma—refer to her beloved. What is the significance? Something wonderful--her husband is her perfume! With these three metaphors, she basically says, "He is what makes me fragrant. He enhances me."

Christ, Our Sachet

Consider first the woman's contentment with her husband being her alluring aroma. What a contrast to the ideals of our culture! "While the king was on his couch, my nard gave forth its fragrance. My beloved is to me a sachet of myrrh…" (1:12–13a). "As He has loved me, I've begun to smell good. He is what makes me beautiful. He is what smells good about me."

Jesus exemplifies this in extraordinary ways. Recall how unlovely we were when he acted to save us. Think about what a stench our sin was in the nostrils of a holy God. We had no redeeming qualities. We were everything abhorrent to holiness. Yet, He poured out His blood, not that He might keep us at arm's length, but—to take His own words from John 14—that He might take us to Himself.[4] We should envision the cross as the price that He paid that He might embrace us for all eternity.

Even at that, He does not leave us in our filth and stench. To those who are redeemed, the gospel says, "For as many of you as were baptized into Christ have put on Christ" (Gal. 3:27). We wear Him. "For our sake he made him to be sin who knew no sin, so that in him we might become the righteousness of God" (2 Cor. 5:21). He took our filth and stench and made it His own so that we might take His righteousness.

If we are beautiful, it is because we are in Him. If we are fragrant, it is because His love lingers on us. He is what smells good about us. This sounds like 2 Corinthians 2:15–16: "For we are the aroma of Christ to God among those who are being saved and among those who are perishing, to one a fragrance from death to death, to the other a fragrance from life to life. Who is sufficient for these things?" His scent lingers on us so that by our godly lives His own are drawn and the world is repulsed. The more we enjoy His love, engaging in fellowship with Him, the stronger that fragrance grows. He is a sachet about our necks.

The worldly impulse to shriek at the notion of a husband's character enhancing the beauty of his wife comes from the same part

---

[4] John 14:3: And if I go and prepare a place for you, I will come again and will take you to myself, that where I am you may be also.

of the fallen human heart that causes us to seek an identity outside of Christ. We are eager to accept the gifts of Christ, but we still contend with the idolatry of self, the desire to make much of "number one."

The world lies to us, offering the devil's counterfeits to make us beautiful and to fix our stench. Yet, it all leads to death. The devil would move us to make much of ourselves. "Here's how you can become beautiful. Here's how you can be attractive. Here's how you can be significant." This is particularly alluring here in the West, where we make so much of the individual. Notice how TV commercials play to our desire to be unique. This drive to be special, to make a name for ourselves, to be the best at something is nothing less than the prideful quest to make much of self. There is nothing wrong with excelling or being different, but to pursue these things for self-elevation or to attain a sense of purpose is tremendously dangerous. It leads us away from true fulfillment in Christ.

How glorious that the woman in the Song is not on a quest to right her off-kilter self-esteem by propping up her sense of personal worth. She finds what she needs in her husband. He is what is attractive about her, she is beautiful to him, and she is content in these things. Oh, that believers would say the same of Christ and that we would find our identity in Him alone and eschew the godless pursuit of an identity outside of Him! Christ-esteem is what will make us full. We can find all that we need in Him.

Indeed, anyone rescued by God who then seeks to find an identity outside of Him will inevitably be led into idolatry. Isn't this the story of ancient Israel? Listen to the prophet Ezekiel tell the story from Yahweh's perspective:

> I made you flourish like a plant of the field. And you grew up and became tall and arrived at full adornment. Your breasts were formed, and your hair had grown; yet you were naked and bare.
> When I passed by you again and saw you, behold, you were at the age for love, and I spread the corner of my garment over you and covered your nakedness; I made my vow to you and entered into a covenant with you, declares the Lord GOD, and you became mine.

Then I bathed you with water and washed off your blood from you and anointed you with oil.

I clothed you also with embroidered cloth and shod you with fine leather. I wrapped you in fine linen and covered you with silk.

And I adorned you with ornaments and put bracelets on your wrists and a chain on your neck.

And I put a ring on your nose and earrings in your ears and a beautiful crown on your head.

Thus you were adorned with gold and silver, and your clothing was of fine linen and silk and embroidered cloth. You ate fine flour and honey and oil. You grew exceedingly beautiful and advanced to royalty.

And your renown went forth among the nations because of your beauty, for it was perfect through the splendor that I had bestowed on you, declares the Lord GOD.

But you trusted in your beauty and played the whore because of your renown and lavished your whorings on any passerby; your beauty became his (Eze. 16:7–15)[5].

Israel became beautiful because of what God did to and for her. Yet, she trusted in her own beauty and was led astray by it. In the wake of God's gracious blessings, she turned her eyes not upward, but inward. The woman of the Song is a wonderful counterpoint, as we should expect, given that the Song is the ideal picture of love. Her husband loves her unconditionally and she becomes lost in him, not herself.

The intended trajectory of the redeemed heart is to say of Christ, "He is what smells good about me." Isn't this what Paul meant in 1 Corinthians 2:2 by proclaiming, "I decided to know nothing among you except Jesus Christ and him crucified"?[6] "For his sake I have suffered the loss of all things and count them as rubbish, in order that I may gain Christ and be found in him…" (Phil. 3:8–9). "Far be it from me to boast except in the cross of our Lord Jesus Christ…" (Gal. 6:14).

---

[5] This is another passage of Scripture pointing to the tendency of the biblical authors to think of the relationship between God and His people as a marriage. The story of Israel is the failed marriage. The story of the Song is the ideal.

[6] One could argue that the entire first four chapters of 1 Corinthians is intended by Paul to make much of Christ and little of himself and others.

"I have been crucified with Christ. It is no longer I who live, but Christ who lives in me" (Gal. 2:20).

One of our biggest temptations is to enjoy others—including God—only to the extent that they make much of us. John Piper asks, "Do you enjoy worshiping God, making much of God, because at the bottom, this God that you're worshiping is committed to making much of you? ...That's idolatry of the worst kind."[7]

Is it possible that the desire for someone to make much of you is what leads you to expect such things from your spouse? People who love themselves intensely expect others to do the same. This is why finding your identity outside of Christ is deadly to marriage. If Christ is your identity, if His righteousness imputed to you is your standing place before God and men, it will not matter what people say about you or how others fail you, even your spouse.

A Sachet, Not an Albatross

Whenever I fly, it amazes me how few passengers are interested in learning how to survive a plane crash. We may have all heard the information before, but surely we could always use a refresher course on how not to die. Yet, while the flight attendants give their survival presentation, some flyers are taking a last desperate drag on their smart phones. Others are dead asleep, as if anesthetic were being piped through the ventilation system. Still others appear frantic to find something—anything—to distract them from the flight attendants.

Among the more crucial pieces of information being missed by the majority of the passengers is how to use the air masks that pop out of the ceiling in the event of cabin depressurization. When those things drop down, what would be the instinct of every parent with a child sitting next to them? "I've got to get the mask on little Johnny—ASAP! Once he's settled, then I'll put on my own." That may be instinctive, but it's the wrong thing to do. Those caring for someone else on a plane should secure their own oxygen mask first. It may sound self-centered, but it's the most caring thing to do. Why? In the event of depressurization, it only takes seconds to black out. If you don't put yours on first, you're in danger of blacking out before you

---

[7] John Piper, "Getting to the Bottom of Your Joy," *Desiring God* (blog), January 3, 2001, https://www.desiringgod.org/messages/getting-to-the-bottom-of-your-joy.

can secure the mask on the other person. Then you're both in serious trouble. By making sure you've got oxygen first, you ensure that you both will be able to breathe.

I've heard people use that illustration to validate a kind of blanket self-interest. "If you don't take care of yourself, you're no good to anyone." "Taking care of yourself" can include virtually anything you want to do, so I'm extremely hesitant to apply the principle to marriage in a broad way, especially when the model given by the Lord Jesus is to pour oneself out for a spouse. However, there is one area of our lives where this principle must be applied if we are going to be a benefit to our spouses. It is in the area of our own spiritual health. To be more specific, if we are not consistently pursuing vibrant fellowship with the Lord, we will not merely be unhelpful to our spouses, but we will drag them down.

J.C. Ryle, in his *Thoughts for Young Men,* addressing the significance of a man's spouse to his spiritual health, wrote, "Your wife must either help your soul or harm it. She will either fan the flame of Christianity in your heart, or throw cold water upon it, and make it burn low. She will either be wings or handcuffs, an encouragement or a hindrance to your Christianity, according to her character."[8] Of course, the same could be said of a husband's influence on his wife's spiritual wellbeing. Your spiritual condition will be either a blessing or a curse to your spouse. If you would be a sachet of myrrh about the neck of your spouse, rather than an albatross, there is one thing you must do for yourself, and therefore for your spouse: wear yourself out pursuing Jesus Christ. In a cultural climate depressurized of the knowledge of God, breathe the pure oxygen of a relationship with Him in Christ.

I, like many of you, have heard more sermons on marriage than I can count. I've been to the marriage conferences and read the books. What I'm proposing here may not sound like the "practical and relevant" advice advertised by so many of these resources. However, take it to the bank: the greatest thing you can do for your spouse is to love Jesus with all your heart, soul, mind, and strength. It is the most practical and relevant course of action to take in your quest for a godly marriage. Avail yourself of the means of fellowship with Jesus and do

[8] J. C. Ryle, *Thoughts For Young Men: Updated Edition With Study Guide,* vol. 1, Christian Manliness Series (Cedar Lake, MI: Waymark, 2018), 54.

so with tireless zeal. Doing so will make you a fragrant aroma around your spouse's neck.

The Means of Fellowship

There are three means of fellowship with Jesus, ways that God has prescribed for enjoying Him. The first is consuming the Word of God in various ways: reading, memorizing, meditating, and listening to teaching/preaching. The Word of God is the voice of Christ in the ear of His bride. We cannot grow in fellowship with Him without it.

The second is prayer. Here is Ryle on prayer as fellowship:

> We must seek to have personal intimacy with the Lord Jesus, and to deal with him as a man deals with a loving friend. We must realize what it is to turn to him first in every need, to talk to him about every difficulty, to consult him about every step, to spread before him all our sorrows, to get him to share in all our joys, to do all as in his sight, and to go through every day leaning on and looking to him…It is ignorance of this way of living that makes so many see no beauty in the Song of Solomon.[9]

Prayer would lend us the ear of the Almighty. Prayer is essential if we would grow in fellowship with Him.

The third means of fellowship is developing meaningful relationships with others in the church. There is a reason the apostles use a human body as a metaphor for the church. We are His hands and feet and voice, doing His work, loving each other on His behalf. According to Ephesians 4:7–16, individual believers grow as all believers use their spiritual gifts in one another's lives. This assumes what Hebrews 10:24–25 commands: meaningful, regular interaction for the purpose of spiritual growth.[10] If we would know more of Christ, we must be engaged in service and fellowship with His body.

---

[9] J. C. Ryle, *Holiness: Its Nature, Hindrances, Difficulties, and Roots* (Carlisle, PA: Banner of Truth Trust, 2014), 128.

[10] Heb. 10:24–25: And let us consider how to stir up one another to love and good works, not neglecting to meet together, as is the habit of some, but encouraging one another, and all the more as you see the Day drawing near.

Two mistakes are typical in the use of these means. The first mistake is using only one or two of these avenues of fellowship. All three must be utilized in order to grow in Christ. They are like three legs on a stool—remove one and the stool falls. Many believers are conscientious about Bible reading and prayer, but without the third leg—meaningful relationships in the church—they do not grow. They end up finding both Bible-intake and prayer to be chores rather than delights.

The second mistake is viewing these means as ends in themselves. They are only means of fellowship with Jesus insofar as they are regarded as such. Bible-reading, prayer, and fellowship with the saints must be conceived of as something like windows through which we see and enjoy a friend—the Lord Jesus. If knowing, desiring, and enjoying Him are not at the center of our motivation for using these means, they will quickly become a drudgery.

The greatest reason to spend time with the Lord is for the wonder of being with Him. It is refreshing and pleasurable. Yet, this gracious Savior will use your time with Him to bless your spouse as well! Consider some of the ways.

Pursuing fulfillment in Jesus prevents the search for identity that tends to stifle a marriage. When you try to find significance outside of the Lord, you will only ever do that in self-centered, idolatrous ways, and you will either expect your spouse to serve that same goal, or you will neglect your spouse while you try to carve out your special corner of the world. However, the satisfaction that comes through fellowship with Jesus makes this an undesirable errand.

Pursuing fellowship with Jesus also destroys the "what have you done for me lately?" mindset. One of my good friends is a fellow elder with me at the church where I serve as the preaching pastor. We get together every other Friday to read the Scriptures, pray, and just talk. I love those Friday mornings because Pastor John rubs off on me. I find myself more joyful, gospel-minded, and zealous for the church because…he's joyful, gospel-minded, and zealous for the church.

The tendency for friends to rub off on us happens also when we spend time with the Lord. Left to ourselves, you and I naturally have a "what have you done for me lately?" mindset. Jesus is the opposite.

He only ever gave of Himself. The more we enjoy fellowship with Him, the more we are taken with Him, the more the Spirit works His character into our hearts. One blessed result is that our spouses are not weighed down by expectations. As Ryle would say, we are not handcuffs for them, but wings.

Pursuing fellowship with Jesus energizes you for His work. Who can deny that this is the case? Who among us has not had the experience of enjoying Him in the Word, prayer, and fellowship with the saints and come away with a greater desire to share Him with others? Jesus Himself modeled this in John 4 in His ministry to the woman at the well. His fellowship with the Father made it so that even though He was exhausted and hungry, He was able to testify, "My food is to do the will of him who sent me and to accomplish his work" (John 4:34). When we experience this fueling for the Lord's work, our spouses are the most immediate beneficiaries.

Pursuing fellowship with Jesus serves as a great boon to your spouse's spiritual life. As mentioned above, we become like the people with whom we spend time. If you are enjoying Jesus and talking about Him and serving alongside Him, that will be contagious in the life of your spouse. By their actions, spouses pursuing the Lord quote Paul, "Be imitators of me, as I am of Christ" (1 Cor. 11:1).

On the other hand, it is absolutely devastating to your spouse when you do not walk closely with the Lord. Rather than a sachet of myrrh, you become the proverbial albatross around the neck. It's an apt metaphor for self-seeking spouses. They don't simply fail to help. They are an impediment to the growth and personal flourishing of their mate, spiritually, emotionally, and every other way. What a tragedy when the Lord has afforded us the means to be a glorious blessing, rather than a burden.

Jesus calls us and enables us to know something better: to love like the man in the Song. We are to love our spouses in such a way that they are not stifled, but helped; not hindered, but enhanced. Marital love enhances the individual. It makes them more than they would be alone. It complements them. The love of the one is a sachet of myrrh about the neck of the other. Christ frees our wills from slavery to sin so that in Him we can live this kind of life.[11]

The husband or wife who wants to be a sachet about the neck of his or her spouse regularly asks the question, "What can I give to my spouse today? How can I love well? What would be a blessing to my beloved?" The first answer to those questions should be, "Pursue Christ." That first answer provides the desire and ability to answer the same questions in many other selfless ways.

The more I'm taken with Jesus, the more I want to be Him to my wife. I've noticed over the years, the closer I stay to Him, the better husband I am. The more I stray from Him, the more I become a miserable wretch of a husband. It has to be all about Him. He is the point. He is the whole reason to care about your marriage.

Discussion Questions/Activities

1. In what things outside of Jesus are you tempted to find your identity?

2. In what ways would finding your identity in Christ represent freedom?

3. Have you ever felt powerless to live sacrificially toward your spouse, as if you were enslaved to self-centeredness? Read Romans 6:1–14. What would Paul say about that "slavery"?

4. Do you currently participate in God's means for fellowship with Jesus? Bible reading, prayer, and fellowship with the saints? If so, to what extent and how often? If not, what prevents you from doing so?

5. In what ways would a growing intimacy with Christ enable you to be a sachet about the neck of your spouse?

---

[11] Rom. 6:4: We were buried therefore with him by baptism into death, in order that, just as Christ was raised from the dead by the glory of the Father, we too might walk in newness of life.

06

SHADE

Respite from the Heat

At about age 25, I went with my wife and extended family to King's Island, a theme park outside of Cincinnati, Ohio. The heat was stifling that day, and I have health issues that cause me to wilt prematurely in the sun. I was beginning to fade about mid-day, so I decided to rest for a few minutes while the others went to another ride. My dad stayed with me. The park was crowded and the only place we could find to sit down was a bench right in the sun. I sat down, but even though there was plenty of room on the bench, my dad continued to stand. I asked him if he wanted to sit, but he just said, "No, I'm fine." It occurred to me that because of where he was standing, he was shading me from the sun. I suspected he was doing this intentionally, so I shifted my weight slightly until my face was in the sun to see what he would do. He shifted his weight as well so that I was shaded once again. He was bearing the sun's glare so that I could get even a small respite from the heat. That was the sweetest shade I ever felt.

My dad's kind act was not surprising. He decided as a young family man that if ever sacrifice was necessary in our home, he would be the one to make it rather than his wife or children. Accordingly, he has always made it easy for me to conceive of God as a loving Father.

Our relief at God's expense—this is a theme of the gospel story woven into many shadows of the Old Testament. Consider the plight of Hagar, sent away by Abraham. Caught in the aftermath of others' bad decisions and exacerbating them herself, she found herself destitute in the wilderness with a son for whom she could not provide. When her water ran out, she resigned herself to Ishmael's death. Yet, though the boy was not the heir of the promise and though Hagar was cast out of the household of promise, God showed kindness, not only in the miraculous appearance of a well, but in promising to prosper her son.[1] Her words at a previous encounter with the Lord proved prophetic: "You are a God of seeing...Truly here I have seen him who looks after me."[2]

This rescue in the wilderness was but a foreshadowing of numerous miraculous interventions by God on behalf of the undeserving. He gave manna, quail, and water from a rock to a nation of perpetual grumblers.[3] He grew a shade tree overnight to comfort a prophet eager to receive grace but loathe to share it.[4] He moved a pagan king to allow the rebuilding of the Jerusalem wall even after the people's first act upon return from exile was to intermarry with the people of the land.[5] God provides relief, rest, and healing to those who do not deserve it.

All of these prefigure the believer's respite in Christ, the ultimate kindness of a generous God toward the unworthy. The human experience is one of heat and pain brought about by sin, but Jesus Himself is a tree of life, bringing shade and healing to the nations.[6]

The Song (1:15–2:7)

(He)

15 Behold, you are beautiful, my love; behold, you are beautiful;
your eyes are doves.

---

[1] Gen. 21:1–20
[2] Gen. 16:13
[3] Exo. 16:12–15, 17:6; Num. 20:8–11
[4] Jonah 4:6
[5] Ezra 9; Neh. 1–2; cf Deut. 7:3
[6] Rev. 22:2

(She)

16 Behold, you are beautiful, my beloved, truly delightful. Our couch is green;

17 the beams of our house are cedar; our rafters are pine.

2:1 I am a rose of Sharon, a lily of the valleys.

(He)

2 As a lily among brambles, so is my love among the young women.

(She)

3 As an apple tree among the trees of the forest, so is my beloved among the young men. With great delight I sat in his shadow, and his fruit was sweet to my taste.

4 He brought me to the banqueting house, and his banner over me was love.

5 Sustain me with raisins; refresh me with apples, for I am sick with love.

6 His left hand is under my head, and his right hand embraces me!

7 I adjure you, O daughters of Jerusalem, by the gazelles or the does of the field, that you not stir up or awaken love until it pleases.

The husband of the Song carries a theme throughout, found again in verse 15: "Behold, you are beautiful, my love; behold, you are beautiful; your eyes are doves." It is significant that he continues to comment on her exceptional beauty because she believes she is common and unattractive. Yet, he is telling her the truth about what he sees when he looks at her, and that truth is changing her. As mentioned in chapter 4, we will see her change in this Song to the extent that she will eventually be described in the same terms that he was described at the beginning of the Song.

She replies in verses 16–17: "Behold, you are beautiful, my beloved, truly delightful. Our couch is green; the beams of our house are cedar; our rafters are pine." She is not just describing an ugly sofa from the '70s. This is garden language. Their couch is a lush garden, not a literal couch. Likewise, their home is not a literal house, but a forest. It's an idealized setting for love.[7] The idea is, "You are delightful; your love has created this glorious atmosphere for our relationship."

Like she did early in the Song, the wife then contrasts his magnificence with her own commonness. The first verse of chapter 2 reads, "I am a rose of Sharon, a lily of the valleys." Many of us associate these phrases with Jesus, yet most of us probably have no idea why. We have simply always heard these phrases used as names for the Lord. The application of these phrases to Jesus can be attributed to the hundreds of years of interpreters allegorizing this text, understanding virtually every element of the text to represent Jesus in some way.

However, this is not the best way to understand these particular phrases. If we attribute these phrases to Jesus, it would be like saying He's nothing special. Scholars are not sure that this Hebrew word should be translated "rose." In fact, the English Standard Version has a note indicating it should probably just be understood as "bulb." We read rose, and think, "Oh, she must be lovely." It's likely that she says, "I'm just a bulb."

"Lily of the valleys" is similar. There are a lot of lilies in the valley. There are a lot of bulbs in Sharon. She's saying, "You are magnificent, I'm common." This is not mere attention-seeking self-deprecation, as if she's angling for a compliment; she is being genuine. She already said these kinds of things about herself in chapter 1. Here, she magnifies him by pointing to her own commonness.

However, he won't allow her to think that she's common: "As a lily among brambles, so is my love among the young women." We could paraphrase, "Okay, you're a lily, but not among lilies—among brambles. Compared to other women, you're a gorgeous flower among thistle weeds." Again, in his eyes she is of exceptional beauty.

She follows suit and makes a comparison of her own about him in verse 3: "As an apple tree among the trees of the forest, so is my beloved among the young men. With great delight I sat in his shadow, and his fruit was sweet to my taste." This is one of the passages that makes me believe that these people are already married. Those who

---

[7] She is preparing us for another metaphor that will be used in chapter 2, where she likens him to an apple tree.

hold that this is an engaged couple typically believe that the marriage takes place in chapter 5. Unfortunately, that leaves us contending with a number of passages, including this one, which certainly sound like these two are enjoying their marital prerogatives. Verses 3-6 are filled with sexual metaphors, virtually identical to those after chapter 5. The easiest explanation is that they are married from the outset.

Consider the significance of what she says in the second half of verse 3: "With great delight I sat in his shadow, and his fruit was sweet to my taste." Context makes this explode. Remember what she said of herself early in chapter 1. Why would a shadow be particularly delightful to her? Because of how harshly the sun treated her as she was out working in the vineyards (1:5-6). His love has offered her a place of protection, perhaps a place of healing, a place where her skin can be renewed from the damage the sun has done to it. "He is just what I need."

"His fruit was sweet to my taste" (2:3). She's been working in the vineyards but has not tended to her own vineyard. From this passage forward, there is the theme of their love being her vineyard. His love has provided her the opportunity to enjoy what she was previously denied—fruit from her own vineyard.

Verse 4 pictures the same thing as verse 3, simply using different words and in reverse order. "He brought me to the banqueting house," is more literally, "He brought me to the house of wine." Remember that the first thing she said to him in chapter 1 was "Your love is better than wine" (1:2). He has brought her, not to a literal banqueting house, but to a private place of marital intimacy. "His banner over me was love" (2:4). Here is another depiction of the shade he provides for her. A banner is a sign, a standard. But it is over her; it shields her, and she explicitly says that it is his love.

So, we have two images in verse 3: shade and fruit. That is, protection and sustenance. The same elements appear in verse 4 as wine and a banner, but in reverse order: sustenance and protection. They appear again in verses 5–6: "Sustain me with raisins; refresh me with apples, for I am sick with love. His left hand is under my head, and his right hand embraces me!" Sustenance in verse 5 and loving protection in verse 6. She rests in his protection and sustenance. In all of this, we get the picture of her basking in his love.

Finally, we come to verse 7, where we find a refrain that will be repeated numerous times in the Song: "I adjure you, O daughters of Jerusalem, by the gazelles or the does of the field, that you not stir up or awaken love until it pleases." Gazelles and does in the Song and in other ancient near Eastern poetry represent the joys of sexual love. The woman is saying to the chorus, "Swear by the joy of sexual love that you will not stir up sexual love until the appropriate time. This is so wonderful, it's well worth waiting for. Wait for it."[8]

The scenes show this: marital love, as God intended, provides shelter and sustenance. "I delighted in his shadow and sat down and his fruit was sweet to my taste."

Christ, Our Shade

Who among us is not like the woman of the Song in the sense that life has wearied us? Like the husband of the Song, Jesus is a tree under whose branches we recline and whose fruit sustains us. "With great delight I sat in his shadow, and his fruit was sweet to my taste" (Song 2:3). If you have known pain—the burning of the proverbial sun—there is no respite, there is no salve, there is no delight like resting in His shadow.

What a glorious picture we find in Psalm 91:

> He who dwells in the shelter of the Most High will abide in the shadow of the Almighty...He will cover you with his pinions, and under his wings you will find refuge; his faithfulness is a shield and buckler...Because you have made the LORD your dwelling place—the Most High, who is my refuge—no evil shall be allowed to befall you, no plague come near your tent... 'Because he holds fast to me in love, I will deliver him; I will protect him, because he knows my name. When he calls to me, I will answer him; I will be with him in trouble; I will rescue

---

[8] Some interpreters would say that she is asking them not to stir up her love. That's a common view among those who believe that this is about an engaged couple. I'm afraid that doesn't make sense. If you don't want your sexual affections to be stirred up, it's not people of the same gender who are usually the problem. That certainly wouldn't have been depicted in an ancient Hebrew poem. A prevalent view among commentators today is that she is exhorting the daughters of Jerusalem to do what she did by saving themselves for marriage.

him and honor him. With long life I will satisfy him and show
him my salvation.'

I was blessed to be raised in the discipline and instruction of the
Lord and taught to believe the Bible is true. Consequently, the
Scriptures are the vocabulary of my mind. I have read the phrases of
the psalms depicting God as a fortress hundreds of times. Yet, recently
during a particularly difficult trial, one phrase of the above psalm
presented itself as if I had never seen or heard it before. "Because you
have made the LORD your dwelling place…" (Psa 91:9).

The other metaphors of structural protection—fortress, shelter,
pinions, wings, refuge—all assume the need for protection.
Conversely, the phrase "dwelling place" indicates habitation
irrespective of circumstances. What a concept--making the Lord our
place of constant habitation. Of course, we are talking about an
omnipresent being, so the psalm is not using literal language. Perhaps
it carries the same idea of the Lord Jesus' sweet prayer that we would
be in Him and in the Father.[9] In those precious last hours with the
disciples, He said, "Abide in me…" (John 15:4). His intention was that
we would remain in close, constant fellowship with Him. The Holy
Spirit likely intended the same in Psalm 91 when inspiring the notion
of God as a dwelling place.

This is one of the great objectives of the gospel. The tabernacle in
the Old Testament was all about God being with His people. It
prefigured Jesus, whom John described as *tabernacling* among us in
John 1:14. The culmination of all things, as depicted by the same
apostle in Revelation 21–22, is that God will dwell with His people.
This is paramount among the reasons to long for eternity.

What a tragedy that so many of us hold Him at arm's length!
Maybe a better way to say it would be, we hold Him at Sunday's length.
We go to church once a week and listen to others read about Him. We
can even hear our own voices singing about Him, but it's like we're
hearing about and singing about a stranger. There is no personal
intimacy or interaction outside of Sunday morning.

---

[9] The "High Priestly Prayer" of John 17, wherein Jesus prayed for us just before His
arrest, is among the most intimate glimpses into the heart of Christ for His bride.

A "Sunday's length" relationship with Jesus is terribly dangerous because it makes us far more susceptible to the false refuges of the world: career, entertainment, food, exercise, hobbies, family, drugs, sex, money. In a million ways, the world, the flesh, and the devil call to us saying, "Come to these things...they'll make you feel better. They'll make you forget about your problems." However, taking refuge in such things is like drinking saltwater when you're dehydrated. It kills you slowly because it distracts you from the fountain of living water.

It's as if Jesus says, "Sit in my shade. Abide in Me. Eat of my fruit. Enjoy fellowship with me. Taste and see that I am good." According to the Lord, our abiding in Him results in our bearing much fruit, thereby glorifying God and proving to be His disciples unto our own ultimate joy (John 15:5, 8, 11). Again, there is a reason that the Holy Spirit inspired sexual metaphors to depict the bliss of fellowship with Christ. Knowing Christ in all His fullness is the highest of pleasures. He calls us to lay aside the world and its counterfeits, allowing Him to be a shadow over our heads.

How do we make this the pattern of our lives? First, we must understand how essential the means of fellowship are that were outlined in the previous chapter. The Word, prayer, and meaningful fellowship with the saints are the tools that the Holy Spirit uses to foster a close, abiding relationship with Jesus. No one will abide in Christ, enjoying His shade, without all three of the means of fellowship.

Second, these means must not represent our panic button used only in times of difficulty. Anyone who has participated in athletics will have heard some form of the saying, "You play like you practice." You cannot expect to perform under stress in ways that have not become habit through voluminous repetition. Growing up, my coaches used the phrase "muscle memory" to refer to the same idea. "You've got to develop muscle memory." Use of the means of fellowship particularly during times of relatively smooth sailing is what develops spiritual muscle memory. If we do not pursue Christ at all times, we will not automatically pursue Him during sustained trouble. Otherwise, in times of intense heat, false refuges may win the day.

Third, when trouble hits, when the sun is blistering us, we must make the conscious decision to turn away from such false refuges and rest in Christ. Our time developing spiritual muscle memory will serve us well during these seasons, providing biblical material to draw upon, familiarity in prayer, and relationships with those who can come alongside us and encourage us. Yet, we must still fight the temptation to look to other things to ease the heat.

Fourth, we must not wish away the difficulties that provide opportunities to put these things into practice. We tend to seek a way of escape from anything unpleasant without considering the tremendous good trials do for us. If it is the case that God forces all things to conform us into the image of Christ, and if trials are the most effective tool at His disposal, we should not be so quick to hit the eject button. The godliest saints among us will count their trials as some of the sweetest times of rest and fellowship with the Lord. They wouldn't necessarily want to relive those trials, but neither would they trade them.

A Shade, Not a Heatwave

You know your spouse. We know the heat he/she has faced and is facing. Did you know that there is no one on the planet better positioned to be shade for your spouse than you? You have the singular blessing of being the most prominent sanctifying influence in his/her life. If your spouse heals from the damage of the sun, if your spouse is refreshed in the Lord, there is no one better positioned to help in that than you are. You are always there, available to encourage and help, pointing to Jesus and coming alongside him/her in prayer.

There are any number of ways you can provide shade for your spouse, but several stand out in light of New Testament teaching. **First, embrace your biblical role as a spouse.** Ephesians 5:22–33 is not merely the most efficient way to run a household. It is the blueprint for living as husband and wife in a manner that commends the gospel. It instructs husbands to spiritually nourish and cherish their wives as their own bodies, pouring themselves out as Christ did for the church. Husbands, give as much care to your wife's well-being as you would to taking care of your own body. Just as you are members of the body of Christ, so you are one flesh with your bride. Be attentive, listening to her. Few are the wives who find no comfort in a husband who listens, prays, watches, and waits with her during storms.

Similarly, wives are commanded to respectfully submit to their husbands as the church submits to Christ in everything. The man who is under a tremendous load endures an even heavier load when he is forced to bear up under the demoralizing influence of a contentious wife. Even the worst of conditions can seem preferable to living with a quarrelsome woman.[10] Frequently, a man's troubles come from outside the home. His wife can help him by minimizing those inside the home.

Second, speak biblical truth at the appropriate time. "Let no corrupting talk come out of your mouths, but only such as is good for building up, as fits the occasion, that it may give grace to those who hear" (Eph. 4:29). Great shade comes from gracious words. That rules out corrupting talk or speech that tears down. If you have a sharp tongue, make Psalm 141:3 your prayer: "Set a guard, O LORD, over my mouth; keep watch over the door of my lips!" Meditate daily on James 3 regarding the terrible power of the tongue. On the other hand, meditate on the healing power of godly words: "Anxiety in a man's heart weighs him down, but a good word makes him glad" (Pro. 12:25). "A word fitly spoken is like apples of gold in a setting of silver" (Pro. 25:11).

Speaking truth at the appropriate time involves knowing what kind of truth is most necessary given your spouse's circumstances. If your spouse is suffering, there is not likely to be a one-size-fits-all biblical response. In 1 Thessalonians 5:14, Paul recommends tailoring the approach to fit the occasion: "And we urge you, brothers, admonish the idle, encourage the fainthearted, help the weak, be patient with them all." Your spouse may be suffering because of his/her own idleness. That is, he/she is lazy in some sense, either physically or spiritually. Others are on the other end of the spectrum, worn-out and discouraged. The apostle calls them, *the fainthearted*. Still others may be suffering simply because they are weak—they don't have the resources to act.

---

[10] Pro. 21:9, 25:24, 27:15–16

These are all different situations, which call for different ways of addressing the needs. It is unhelpful at best, devastating at worst to bring the wrong remedy to bear on someone who needs assistance. For example, if you give to a lazy person the kind of help that you would to the weak, you are just enabling them in their laziness. Paul says the idle person needs to be rebuked. This could take the form of a gentle, "Look, this is ungodly idleness. You need to get busy obeying the Lord." If they are spiritually lazy, show them from the Scriptures what happens to the person who does not keep a close watch on his or her life. There are plenty of passages in Proverbs, particularly the passages on wisdom and folly in chapters 8–9. If they are physically lazy, you could share with them 2 Thessalonians 3 where Paul said that those who don't work shouldn't eat.[11] The idle person needs to be lovingly rebuked.

How could rebuking the idle offer them shade? It is unkind to allow someone to continue in their sin. Sin is costly in that it robs us of the comfort, joy, and peace afforded by close fellowship with Jesus.[12] Loving confrontation seeks to bring them back to fellowship with God and man. It is a kindness all too often withheld.

On the other hand, if you rebuke the discouraged the way you would the idle, you will likely drive them deeper into discouragement. Encourage them from the Scriptures. Read to them from the psalms those great prayers of needy people to a great and kind God.[13] Bring the biblical treatment appropriate to the situation, and thereby offer shade to your spouse.

Third, be patient. This is the final exhortation of 1 Thessalonians 5:14. No matter what your spouse's circumstances, be patient. We may want to "help" our spouses with their suffering by prodding them to get over it, motivated mainly by our own convenience. Their difficulty is a major annoyance to us, so we push them to get a handle on it. Can you imagine Jesus being that way? "Get this fixed because you're driving me nuts! This problem you have is getting in my way." No, in our sin He pities us because He knows

---

[11] Or 1 Tim. 5:8, if someone does not provide for the members of his household, "he has denied the faith and is worse than an unbeliever."

[12] Psa. 51, 66:18; 1 Pet. 3:7

[13] To name a few: Psa. 3, 34, 40, 63, 91, 103, 121

we're miserable. So He helps us. Purpose that your spouse will feel no heat from you in the form of, "Hey, your suffering is cramping my style."

Fourth, make your spouse's burdens your own. There is a young husband and father in the church I pastor. As I've watched him over the years, I have begun to pray, "Lord, please send two just like him to marry my daughters." He exemplifies the idea of bearing his spouse's burdens. To my knowledge, his blessed wife has not faced a trial alone since the day she married this man. He has shepherded her through conflicts with others, spent himself caring for her in sickness, and stayed close to Christ so as to better serve her. If you ask this man the state of his wife's heart or what concerns her on any given day, he'll tell you instantly because he has adopted her concerns as his own.

"Bear one another's burdens, and so fulfill the law of Christ" (Gal. 6:2). This is the opposite mindset to that of the impatient observer, addressed above. If we are truly one flesh with our spouses, there should be no "his and hers" problems. We must enter into the suffering of our spouses. The Lord did this when He took on human flesh, was tempted in every way as we are, made our sin His own, died for it, and dedicated Himself eternally to interceding for us![14] To be shade for your spouse, as Christ is shade for you, grab those burdens and own them.

Fifth, serve your spouse. Paul argues in the book of Galatians that freedom from the law does not equal freedom from serving others. Rather, love will lead us to serve.[15] Making your spouse's burdens your own will make you naturally in-tune with your spouse's needs. Love will move you to meet those needs. When he/she needs a listening ear, give it. When he/she needs sexual fulfillment, offer it. When he/she needs prayer, get on your knees together. When he/she needs rest, move heaven and earth to provide a quiet, uninterrupted place.

Certainly, there are other ways to be shade for your spouse, but these represent a great starting point. Failing to do these things will not merely deny them the shade that you otherwise could give, but will

---

[14] Phil. 2:5–8; Heb. 4:15; 2 Cor. 5:21; 1 Pet. 2:24; Heb. 7:25; Rom. 8:34
[15] Gal. 5:13

intensify their difficulty. Have you been an influence that has only intensified the pain and suffering of your spouse? Has your presence in impeded their growth in Christ, or healing from hurts? Have you added to the sun's damage to her skin? If he/she has grown in Him, has it been in spite of you?

Oh, to be like Christ for them! What a wonderful Savior! Consider what a glorious thing it would be for your spouse to be able to say, "My spouse has been the tangible expression of Christ's shade in my life. With great delight I sit in my spouse's shadow and rest. He/she is my safe place, and the fruit is sweet to my taste. My spouse is a gift of the Lord Jesus, helping me pursue Him."

Discussion Questions/Activities

1. Since you read the last chapter, what new habits have you instituted regarding the means of fellowship (Bible, prayer, fellowship with the saints)?

2. What relationships have you begun to build with other believers for the sake of meaningful fellowship? If there are none, who could you approach?

3. What are the false refuges that typically pull at you during difficult times? (Think about the activities, mental and physical, that you engage in to ease your stress.)

4. Think through the recent trials in your spouse's life. In what specific ways did you offer shade? In what specific ways did you intensify the heat? If necessary, repent and seek forgiveness.

5. Identify with your spouse ways that you both can grow in the area of offering shade to one another.

07

CALLING & CATCHING

A Dual Invitation

My wife and I have always been conscientious about maintaining closeness in our relationship. We have very little tolerance for disconnectedness and have employed different strategies over the years to stay close to one another, including scheduling time for everyday conversations and regular date nights. Even when money has been very tight, we've made time for "couch dates"--evenings where the kids are banished from the basement while the two of us talk, share a meal, and watch a movie together.

This intentionality to stay close is essential, but not enough. Prior to my writing this book, I preached a sermon series on the Song of Songs at our church. One might assume that this season would occasion wonderful times of intimacy on all levels in our marriage. Certainly, the Song invites us to deeper marital closeness. At the same time, the enemy knows this. We can and should think of our pursuit of closeness as both an invitation to our spouses to know us more deeply *and an invitation to the enemy to work us over.* We should extend the one while being wary of the other.

A few weeks before I started preaching the Song, my wife, Shelby, said, "We need to be careful. Satan is probably going to attack our marriage more during this series than he ever has with any other series you've preached." I said, "Wow, you're right." My preparation for the series did move us to think about important things, but the need to keep a close watch for attack eventually slipped our minds.

The week after the first sermon in the series, Shelby and I had a date planned with other couples from church. Just before we were supposed to leave, a nuclear bomb of a fight erupted between us, and we left the house angry at each other. We fought half the way to our destination. During a moment of silence, I said, "The devil is going to destroy us during this sermon series." Shelby told me later she had been thinking, "Well, I'm not the one who decided to preach the Song of Songs, Pal!" The second half of the drive took place in complete silence as we fumed.

When we arrived at the venue, I'm sure steam billowed out of the vehicle as we opened the doors. Unfortunately, this wasn't just a simple dinner out. The purpose of this little get-together was to take ballroom dancing lessons. It was terrible. Our friends from church had a wonderful time; we were miserable. Furious with one another, we didn't even want to be in the same room, much less spend the evening in a close embrace, dancing. We've since reconciled, of course. The next day we repented and forgave one another. We would now love to learn how to dance without clenched teeth.

We were aware of the danger at first, but intimacy that endures must not only be pursued, but also protected. It does not just happen, and it will not preserve itself. Intimacy is an invitation that must be constantly extended. This is true in the spiritual realm and in marriage. Part of this endeavor is to recognize that the enemy would answer the invitation as well, so as to spoil what God has wrought. We must simultaneously invite closeness and be prepared for danger.

The Song (2:8–17)

(She)

8 *The voice of my beloved! Behold, he comes, leaping over the mountains, bounding over the hills.*

9 *My beloved is like a gazelle or a young stag. Behold, there he stands behind our wall, gazing through the windows, looking through the lattice.*

10 *My beloved speaks and says to me: "Arise, my love, my beautiful one, and come away,*

11 for behold, the winter is past; the rain is over and gone.

12 The flowers appear on the earth, the time of singing has come, and the voice of the turtledove is heard in our land.

13 The fig tree ripens its figs, and the vines are in blossom; they give forth fragrance. Arise, my love, my beautiful one, and come away.

14 O my dove, in the clefts of the rock, in the crannies of the cliff, let me see your face, let me hear your voice, for your voice is sweet, and your face is lovely.

(Both)

15 Catch the foxes for us, the little foxes that spoil the vineyards, for our vineyards are in blossom."

(She)

16 My beloved is mine, and I am his; he grazes among the lilies.

17 Until the day breathes and the shadows flee, turn, my beloved, be like a gazelle or a young stag on cleft mountains.

In this passage, we see the husband's love for his wife through her eyes. She recounts his pursuit of her, recites his invitation to her, and shares her answer to him. His love is on display; her perception is the window.

"The voice of my beloved! Behold, he comes, leaping over the mountains, bounding over the hills. My beloved is like a gazelle or a young stag. Behold, there he stands behind our wall, gazing through the windows, looking through the lattice" (2:8–9). The intensity of the man's love for the woman is on display here. Based upon her appraisal of him and herself earlier, observers might consider him out of her league. He's so objectively desirable that all the young women are attracted to him and praise him at the beginning. At the same time, she is culturally unattractive. Therefore, one might expect this to be a relationship where he leaves it to her to pursue him. After all, she's lucky to be with him.

Yet, this passage shows that that is not the case. He is after her, eager for her love! She hears his voice calling, sees him looking for her, and likens him to a gazelle or a young stag. Picture a young buck during mating season.[1] He's on a mission. All of his overtures in the previous passage about her exceptional beauty were not merely to make her feel better. He genuinely finds her attractive and desirable.

Next, his words are found, but quoted by her: "My beloved speaks and says to me: 'Arise, my love, my beautiful one, and come away…'" (2:10). He voices his desire for intimacy in the form of an invitation, pursuing her. This line is like the first of two bookends in this paragraph. The same words come at the end of verse 13. Why should she come away? She quotes him: "'For behold, the winter is past; the rain is over and gone…'" (2:11). The time for waiting is over. Perhaps this is something of a reference to her words to the daughters of Jerusalem in 2:7. The woman said to them, "Don't stir up or awaken love until it pleases. Do what I did; wait until marriage." He's saying, "We've done our waiting."

She continues her quotation: "'The flowers appear on the earth, the time of singing has come, and the voice of the turtledove is heard in our land. The fig tree ripens its figs, and the vines are in blossom; they give forth fragrance. Arise, my love, my beautiful one, and come away…'" (2:12–13). Recall her words in 1:14, "Our couch is green." This language about springtime blooming is a reference to their blooming "vineyards", their physical desire. He's saying, "It's time to

---

[1] This passage, among others, has strong sexual overtones. Are we ignoring them by not majoring on the sexual themes? No. There are two reasons to regard the sexual imagery as pointing to more than mere physical union. First, the love depicted in the Song is ideal marital love. To take the sexual imagery as strictly pointing to the physical aspect of marriage would be to understand ideal marital love to be largely sexual in nature. There are indicators throughout the Song that these two people are not just after the physical. There is something deeper going on between these two. That deeper intimacy is expressed in sexual union. In the Song, sexual intimacy represents the fullness of marriage.

Second, because the Song is intended to be read Christologically, the sexual imagery is obviously metaphorical. As has been mentioned in earlier chapters, sexual imagery is used to represent the love of Christ because sexual union is the highest of earthly pleasures.

Therefore, we're not ignoring the text. We're getting at the real intent of the text, which is not simply the surface-level imagery. Still, this does not rule out application to the sexual relationship in marriage, which is a component of the totality of intimacy that the sexual imagery is intended to address.

enjoy one another. Don't you feel it?" He's calling her to enjoy relations with him, the physical expression of their whole relationship.[2]

"O my dove, in the clefts of the rock, in the crannies of the cliff, let me see your face, let me hear your voice, for your voice is sweet, and your face is lovely" (2:14). There's no beating around the bush here. Where the English Standard Version reads, "let me see your face," a more literal translation would be, "show me your appearance." One Hebrew scholar renders it, "Show me your form."[3] In other words, he doesn't just want to look at her face.

Yet, he is not only after her body. He also says, "Let me hear your voice, for your voice is sweet" (2:14). He wants to talk to her, as well. The whole scene shows him calling for her, wooing her to come and enjoy the richness of their intimacy together.

Her recollection of his invitation is interrupted in verse 15: "Catch the foxes for us, the little foxes that spoil the vineyards, for our vineyards are in blossom." What might sound like a diversion from the invitation is truly an essential preservative to their intimacy. The two exhort one another to "catch the foxes."[4] The command is to protect the intimacy of the relationship. It is as if they are saying, "Our vineyards are in bloom, ripe for intimacy, and the little foxes are a

---

[2] This is another text indicating that they are married. This would be highly inappropriate language to exchange between two unmarried people.

[3] Duane A. Garrett and Dr. Paul R House, *Song of Songs and Lamentations*, vol. 23B, Word Biblical Commentary (Grand Rapids: Zondervan, 2018), l. 5380.

[4] There is not widespread agreement among commentators regarding who utters this verse. The difficulty lies in that the verb is a plural imperative. Multiple people are being told to catch the foxes. Some believe that this is still the man speaking to the woman (or her recitation of his words). Others believe that the woman speaks to the man. Again, the problem with these two options is that it is a plural imperative. One would not use a plural imperative to tell one person to do something. For this reason, other commentators believe that either the man or the woman is speaking to the chorus telling them to catch the foxes. Still others hold that this is the chorus saying to the man and woman, "Hey, catch the foxes because our vineyards (the vineyards of the chorus) are in bloom."

These options are just as problematic as the former. Why would the man or the woman invite the chorus to help them protect their vineyard, especially when we understand the vineyard to be a reference to their sexual relationship? Likewise, why would the chorus invite the man and the woman to help them protect their vineyard, especially when in 2:7 the woman has essentially told them to go take a cold shower until they were married? It seems to me that the least problematic option is that the husband and wife say this line to one another.

threat, so let us catch the foxes and keep them from ruining our intimacy." To catch the foxes is to deal with those things that threaten marital closeness.

In verse 16, the woman speaks: "My beloved is mine, and I am his; he grazes among the lilies."[5] This may be the sweetest verse in the whole song. It is as if she is pinching herself to think that this is true. "This wonderful man desires me, has given himself to me. And I get to give myself to him." She is commenting on what his pursuit of her means. "My beloved belongs to me. I belong to my beloved. His heart is mine and mine is his." Given the context, we should understand this to mean, "My beloved is mine to enjoy, and I am my beloved's to enjoy."

In verse 17, she gives her response to his call: "Until the day breathes and the shadows flee, turn, my beloved, be like a gazelle or a young stag on cleft mountains." The young woman answers the call of her husband in the affirmative. "Until the day breathes and the shadows flee," is a poetic way of saying, "Yes, let's enjoy one another all night long." Her invitation for him to be like a gazelle or young stag on cleft mountains means, "Yes, I want what you want. I want to be intimate with you."

The Song depicts a love that calls for and welcomes vibrant intimacy. It doesn't wait for the other partner to act. It woos and pursues. It is also a love that safeguards intimacy. It does not sit back and watch as the foxes ruin the vineyards. It catches them to preserve the vineyards.

Christ, Our Pursuer

Some believers conceive of Jesus' disposition toward the Church as something like that of the handsome jock taking his little sister's annoying friend to the prom as a favor. Nothing could be further from the truth. Like the husband in the Song, Jesus genuinely desires His bride. Consider all that He has done to be with us!

---

[5] "Grazing among the lilies" is an image building upon the idea of the husband as a gazelle or young stag. It is another phrase making it very difficult to hold that these are two engaged people and not two married people. Early in the passage he was gazing, but now he is grazing. Early in the passage he was leaping over the hills, but in verse 17 he is invited to be on the hills. They're married.

First, Jesus atoned for our sin at the steepest of costs. He condescended, becoming a man, embracing all the challenges and temptations associated with our humanity, so that He could fulfill the law of God on our behalf and take the penalty for our sin on the cross. For thirty-three years, He bore the full weight of temptation without giving in.[6] For six hours, He bore the omnipotent wrath of His own Father, eventually declaring our debt paid in full.[7] Being raised from the dead, He has now ascended to the Father where He ever lives to pray for us.[8] Just as the blood of Abel called out for judgment, so the blood of Christ calls out for atonement unto reconciliation and fellowship.[9] Has anyone ever paid more to gain and keep a bride?

Second, He powerfully called us to Himself. There was a horrible time when in our fallenness we could not see His desirability, when we loved only our darkness, burdened by sin, death, and hell.[10] It was like the time of the winter and rain depicted in verse 11. Yet, as the husband calls to his beloved, so Christ called to us: "Come to me, all who labor and are heavy laden, and I will give you rest. Take my yoke upon you, and learn from me, for I am gentle and lowly in heart, and you will find rest for your souls. For my yoke is easy, and my burden is light" (Matt. 11:28–30). He called us to intimacy through the preaching of the gospel.[11] He left no possibility that we would not be His.[12] He came and claimed us for His own, changing our hearts and bringing us to repentance and faith, so tenacious is this Lover of souls![13]

Third, He provided means of fellowship with Him. We've considered this before, but rather than focus on the simple reality of these means, consider the lengths to which Jesus has gone to give them to us. The Word of God is perhaps the most extravagant gesture of love imaginable…outside of the cross. It is the most intricately woven,

---

[6] Heb. 2:18; 4:15

[7] John 19:30; cf Col. 2:13–14

[8] Heb. 7:25; Rom. 8:34

[9] Heb. 12:24

[10] Eph. 2:1–3, 4:18; cf John 8:43 (NASB): "Why do you not understand what I am saying? It is because you cannot hear My word."

[11] Rom. 10:17

[12] John 6:37; 10:14–16, 26–30

[13] Eze. 36:26; Eph. 2:8; Phil. 1:29; 2 Tim. 2:25

error-free tapestry ever created. It has been given to us for one reason: that we might know God in Christ. Likewise, prayer is a precious gift. It was highly costly. Jesus bought our access to the Father with His blood. We can speak to the Creator Almighty because Jesus bore His wrath for us. The third means—fellowship with the saints—is easily the most overlooked gift. In it, Jesus gives to the Church what is most precious to Him—the Church! It was the Spirit of Christ who inspired the words of Psalm 16:3: "As for the saints in the land, they are the excellent ones, in whom is all my delight." The Church exists as the hands, feet, and voice of Jesus in our lives. We lack no good thing necessary to enjoy fellowship with Jesus. He has made sure of it.

Fourth, He assures us of our rightful place with Him. Some evangelicals wrongly view the converted, justified, believing bride of Christ as a filthy, wretched whore. They think of themselves as the proverbial elephant in the throne room of God. There are multiple problems with this, the greatest of which is that it tends to take passages that speak of our former lostness and read them into our current state of justification. It is true that we were filthy, wretched whores.[14] Yet, because of the imputed righteousness of Christ, before God we are that way no more. According to 1 Corinthians 6:9–11, we *were* sexually immoral, idolaters, adulterers, homosexuals, thieves, drunkards, revilers, swindlers. That *was* our identity. We *were* unworthy to inherit the kingdom of God. But that past tense verb is precisely the point: "Such *were* some of you. But you were washed, you were sanctified, you were justified in the name of the Lord Jesus Christ and by the Spirit of our God" (1 Cor. 6:11).

If we truly grasped that, how could we stay seated and not shout, "Amen"? Yes, we still sin, but we are not what we were, and He does not see us the same way that He did. Romans teaches that we were enemies, but now we are children.[15] Ephesians reminds us that we were far off, but now we have been brought near by the blood of Christ.[16] To be sure, we are not what we will be, but we are not what we were. Jesus assures us that we belong to Him and with Him.

---

[14] References to spiritual whoredom abound in the Scriptures. Just a sample: Num. 15:38–39; Deut. 31:16; Psa. 106:39; Jas. 4:4; 1 Pet. 4:3
[15] Rom. 5:10, 8:15
[16] Eph. 2:11–13

Jesus is not like a bridegroom who has married down, who knows that He is way out of His bride's league, and who therefore puts all responsibility on her to pursue Him, as if to say, "You're so lucky to be with me. If you want to spend time with me, you know where I am." We ought not conceive of the risen Christ as being able to take us or leave us. He is not indifferent toward His bride. Christ has paid an enormous price to be able to say, "Arise, my love, my beautiful one, and come away!"

As we read in the Song, we should hear the heart of Christ saying to the church, "Show me your appearance, let me hear your voice; for your voice is sweet, and your appearance is lovely." Some of us are afraid to think this way because we are scared to death that this is going to lead to man-centered thinking or a lax disposition toward sin. However, let's look to the woman of the Song for the appropriate response. As the man loves her well and is taken with her beauty, she does not become enthralled with herself, but she becomes enamored with him. That is what the Song should do in our hearts toward Christ.

We must be beautiful to Christ; our voices must be sweet to Him—He shed His own blood to make this so. Our beauty is His beautiful, imputed righteousness. This should even make us quick to confess our sins to Him. He accepts us not because of what we have done and are, but because of what He has done and is. Therefore, there is no reason to hide in shame. His love covers us. When our voices extol Him, there can be nothing sweeter to His ears.

My beloved is mine and I am His. He is mine to enjoy and I am His to enjoy. Do you think of Jesus as a person to enjoy? Conceiving of Him that way does not denigrate Him or lower Him. This is precisely how the Bible presents Him to us, as a person, as a brother, as a bridegroom. If we understood the wonders of His person, we would be like the woman of this Song, saying to the Lord, "Yes, Lord, I want what you want. Until the day breathes and the shadows flee, let us enjoy fellowship."

Christ, Our Protector

Anyone who has been a believer for long knows that there are those little foxes seeking to ruin the Vineyard. We might associate these little foxes with the world, the flesh, and the devil. Certainly, these enemies seek to spoil our intimacy with Jesus. However, perhaps it would be best to associate the little foxes with the subtler dangers that we are not so apt to recognize. There could be any number of them, and there may be some unique to each of us. In this section, I would like to propose a few that you may never have considered.

First, we must beware of equating ministry with intimacy with the Lord. It is quite possible to wear ourselves out serving in the local church without having any kind of closeness with Jesus. The Lord even warned that there will be those on the last day claiming ministry tasks as evidence of their salvation to whom He will reply, "I never knew you; depart from me, you workers of lawlessness" (Matt. 7:23). What a deadly little fox is this brand of self-deception. It convinces believers that they are growing when they are really stagnant. It convinces dead sinners that they are glory bound.

Among believers, it can happen so slowly and unintentionally that all of a sudden you find yourself spiritually exhausted. I have experienced it myself. A few years ago, I was completely burned out in ministry. I described the state of my heart to my fellow elders using the words "dull" and "dry." How could this be? As the main teacher in our congregation, I spent far more time in the Word than anyone else in the church! The Lord showed me that ministry tasks—even the preparation of sermons—do not equal fellowship with the Lord. I had slowly developed a conception of the Bible as raw materials for sermons and Bible studies rather than food for my own soul! The remedy was to build a thick wall between my own devotional time and my preparation for ministry responsibilities.

The enemy loves this little fox. When we are busy with kingdom work, it is simple to convince ourselves that busyness in ministry equals spiritual health. It does not.

Second, we must beware of boredom. How could boredom be so dangerous? Nature abhors a vacuum. Boredom represents just such a void, but one which is emotional and mental in nature. If it is not intentionally and quickly filled with godly pursuits, it will be filled naturally and automatically with our basest interests and affections.

John Calvin wrote, "The human mind is, so to speak, a perpetual forge of idols."[17] There is a spiritual principle at work here that is reflected in such passages as Romans 1:18–32 and Matthew 12:43–45. At his core, man is a worshipper. Because of the Fall, he defaults to false worship. Right worship requires intentionality and effort. Because boredom is something like a state of mental and emotional passivity, it is fertile ground for "idol forging."

The enemy is poised to ruthlessly take advantage of boredom. He does so by offering a rescue from it in the form of interesting or stimulating thoughts and activities. They may not be inherently sinful, but they are designed to distract us from the Lord and eventually dominate our attention.[18]

Catching this fox entails recognizing boredom for what it is and filling our time with godly pursuits. Some of us may be so busy that we cannot imagine having a spare moment that is not filled with some task or necessary thought. However, even the busiest of us will sooner or later have this little fox nipping at our heels. We must be prepared. What will you do to fill your thoughts and time when the need arises?

Third, we must beware of spiritual hobby horses. A hobby horse is a topic to which one is constantly drawn. A spiritual hobby horse then is an issue or doctrine about which we may become passionate, distractedly so, to the extent that it diverts us from what is truly important. It is fine to have diverse convictions within the church, but we must realize that our convictions and spiritual interests must be subordinated to the Lordship of Christ for the good of our own spiritual health and that of the church as a whole.

Paul warned Titus to "avoid foolish controversies, genealogies, dissensions, and quarrels about the law, for they are unprofitable and worthless" (Titus 3:9). Was it that Paul didn't want any theological discussion taking place? Was Titus being instructed to abstain from all theological contention? Certainly not, for in the same letter, Paul instructed Titus to appoint elders who were steeped in the Scriptures and able to rebuke and correct those who contradict.[19] It is simply that

---

[17] John Calvin, *Institutes of the Christian Religion*, Book 1.XI.8-9.

[18] 2 Cor. 11:3: But I am afraid that as the serpent deceived Eve by his cunning, your thoughts will be led astray from a sincere and pure devotion to Christ.

[19] The apostle gave the same instruction to Timothy—1 Tim. 1:3–7, 6:3–5.

there are some issues that should be first-tier concerns of the church, others second-tier, third-tier, and so on. Yet, no matter on what tier a particular spiritual issue, concern, interest, or doctrine falls, it is possible for that issue to become inordinate in our attention so that we neglect intimacy with the Lord.

I have known people to be so concerned about eschatology—the legitimately biblical doctrine of the end times—that they have difficulty holding conversations about anything else. They have even more difficulty holding *civil* conversations with those who disagree with them about eschatology!

We should even be cautious about our conception of the appropriate place of theology itself. I serve in a church where right theology is a high priority because if we don't understand God rightly we cannot worship Him rightly. That connection between theology and worship must be maintained both in the congregation and in the life of the individual believer. A subtle, cunning little fox would love to make theology itself the object of worship in the hearts of many believers. I regret that I have been among them in the past. The Lord graciously woke me from that deadly slumber and helped me to see that theology is only helpful in that it helps me to know Him.

Spiritual hobby horses can take many forms along the spectrum from relatively unimportant topics to quite essential doctrines. The enemy is so nefarious that he will use any of them to distract us from devotion to the Lord. Theology (truth) must lead to doxology (worship). I have been excited about doctrines as ends in themselves and allowed them to lead me away from the Lord. Those same doctrines, when used as avenues for worship, have been critical to my spiritual growth. It is essential to remember that mere passion for a spiritual issue is not passion for Jesus. He and He alone must be Lord of all.

These and other foxes are on the prowl as we speak, but if we truly belong to Christ, the Bridegroom will not allow us to stray for long. He catches the foxes, and He has called us to do the same. To that end, He has put the Holy Spirit inside of us along with a God-given conscience to pull us back to Him when we stray. We have a responsibility to join Him in catching the foxes. The commands and warnings of the New Testament are intended to move us to keep a close watch on our own hearts so that we would not stray from Him, but always grow in our affection for Him.

Pursuing & Preserving Intimacy

We're really good at pursuing intimacy with our spouses in the beginning, aren't we? We're great at securing a mate, but the pursuit of intimacy tends to go downhill after the wedding. Yet, look at how tenaciously Jesus has pursued and continues to pursue us. To depict the gospel well, we must pursue intimacy at all levels from the altar to the grave.

This is not as mundane as going on dates and romantic getaways. Those are good things, but they do not equal pursuing intimacy. You can have a date night every night and go to Hawaii three times a year, yet be no more intimate with one another than you were before you started. Think of those as occasions for intimacy.

Some of you feel like your marriage is stale. You haven't shared any meaningful experience in a long time. There's not much closeness. What should you do?

Invite your spouse to know you. Share your thoughts. Share your concerns, your struggles, your hopes. Most of us live in two worlds. We live in our own mind and heart, and we live in the external world. We have our own thoughts, struggles, hopes, and concerns, but for the most part those are kept to ourselves in secret.

Our outward lives can look very different. We may manufacture a completely different persona for everyone else to see. Invite your spouse to know the real you. Do that by volunteering that information. Trust them with those things.

Press into knowing your spouse. Seek his/her intimate thoughts. Ask questions. Inquire about his/her concerns, struggles, and hopes. When your spouse shares those things, adopt them to the extent that you empathize and pray about them. Enter into your spouse's struggles by helping with them.

Live out your one-flesh relationship on every level. God has joined you together profoundly. Talk about personal things. Talk about the Lord. Talk about how you are doing spiritually. Talk about the Bible. Pray together about the things on your mind. And let your sexual union be the culmination of the closeness of every other area of the marriage.

In other words, don't do life by yourself. Call to your spouse. "Arise, my love, my beautiful one, and come away" (Song 2:10). Woo your spouse to come to a place of deeper knowledge of you and pursue a deeper knowledge of your spouse. Don't allow your one-flesh relationship to be expressed only in the realm of the flesh. Share everything.

Commit to catching the foxes. The enemy loves gospel-defaming Christian marriages, so he sends little foxes into the vineyards. What are some of these foxes? **One is spiritual complacency.** Nothing will threaten your intimacy more than flagging intimacy with the Lord. You simply cannot enjoy marriage in all of its fullness while not pursuing Christ in all his fullness. Why? Because you need Him and His strength in order to be the spouse you're called to be. It's somewhat silly to be concerned about your marriage, when your relationship with the Lord is an afterthought. If you want to enjoy a marriage of rich intimacy, pursue Christ with reckless abandon.

Another common fox that ruins vineyards is unreconciled hurt. We'll have occasion to consider this more in later chapters. For now, just know that if you're in the habit of not resolving conflicts biblically, your marriage is going to be doomed to shallow levels of intimacy. You won't trust each other, share intimate details of your life with one another, be drawn to one another, or serve one another.

Some couples have unreconciled issues that go back years. Keep this in mind: time does not heal all wounds. If you have unreconciled issues, your vineyard is ripe for the foxes of bitterness that are going to strip it of any meaningful expressions of godly love. In some cases, catching the foxes may be as simple as just confessing sin, repenting, and seeking forgiveness. In other cases, you may need biblical counseling. Whatever the situation, there is hope and help in Christ. Don't just sit there and let the foxes destroy the vineyard.

Another common fox ruining the vineyard is busyness. It is all too common to allow unessential things to crowd out essential things. The pursuit of intimacy takes intentionality. If you're someone who prizes spontaneity, and you're relying on spontaneity to keep the intimacy alive in your marriage, you're going to be disappointed. The foxes of busyness are going to choke out the intimacy. If you find it difficult to have meaningful conversations, put them on the calendar. If you find it difficult to find time to come together sexually, put it on the calendar. If necessary, remove from your lives some of these unnecessary things so that there is time for what is necessary. Deep intimacy in marriage is biblically necessary.

Another common fox is allowing other relationships to take a higher priority than that of your spouse. Sometimes it's the children, sometimes it's extended family, sometimes it's friends, sometimes it's coworkers. Consider this: the Bible describes none of those relationships as a one-flesh union. You are in a one-flesh union with one person on this planet—your spouse. That is your primary human relationship. All other human relationships, including your children, should be subordinated to your relationship with your spouse.

A Glorious Spectacle

Finally, consider the gospel-commending power and spectacle of two people living out verse 16: "My beloved is mine, and I am his." In a world where strife is rampant in marriage, what does it say when two people are seen enjoying knowing one another? They serve one another, obviously care for one another, and adopt one another's concerns. They are helplessly affectionate with one another. They have eyes for only one another. In a society where no one is satisfied with anything, and where everything—including a marriage—can be sent back and traded in for a better model, what does a Song of Songs kind of marriage say? There is a principle at work in these two that is other-worldly. If those two people are faithful to speak the gospel with their mouths, their marriage will not only act it out, but it will prove its veracity.

Further, the glorious wonder of it all is that they will enjoy its full delights in the process. Christ calls to us to join Him. He exhorts us to catch the foxes. Let's do so, and let's emulate Him in our marriages.

Discussion Questions/Activities

1. Discuss with your spouse the evidences that Christ desires His bride. Which of those mentioned in the chapter is most meaningful to each of you? Why?

2. Which foxes are threatening your fellowship with the Lord? What is the best way to deal with them?

3. What are the foxes threatening your intimacy with your spouse? Sit down and discuss them together.

   a. Are one or both of you succumbing to spiritual complacency? How can you help one another with this?

   b. Do you share unreconciled hurts in the recent or distant past? What are these hurts? Confess and seek one another's forgiveness.

   c. Is busyness plaguing your intimacy? What specifically is getting in the way? Discuss together practical ways to make time for conversation, prayer, and sexual intimacy.

   d. Are other relationships taking priority over your marriage? What can and should be done?

08

DESPERATE & DISABUSED

Buying Fairy Tales

Romantic comedies can be a tool of Satan.

This has nothing to do with the fact that I find them torturous. Think about what they do to us. Rather, think about how they play on our sinfulness. Before we get married, we watch the rom-coms and *swoon*. They make us love *love*. We get excited about the possibility of finding someone like the perfect man or woman depicted in the movie. "I can't wait for someone to make me feel like that!" They are modern day fairy tales, typically pushing a myth of perfect compatibility and easy harmony—exactly what our sinful hearts believe we deserve. Sure, each movie might present one or two hiccups in the relationship, but the fix is usually simple and the happiness immediate.

Many of us have a whole different reaction to rom-coms a few years after we get married. We still swoon…until the credits roll. Then we get angry—not at Hollywood, but at our spouses for failing to be the person in the movie. We think, even if we don't say it, "You don't make me feel like that." We know we've just watched a fictional story, but we truly believe we deserve the fairy tale.

The world, under the influence of the god of this world, is eager to provide these fairy tales that the flesh desires, and not only in the arena of love. Because of our fallen natures, we want others to make much of us and to make our lives easy. The enemy sells the fairy tale by telling us what our sinful ears want to hear: "Yes, you deserve it; you're worth it; life doesn't have to be so hard."

Fad diets exist because we want to believe it's possible to be healthy without discipline and self-control. Internet scammers abound because of how simple it is to play on our desire for quick money with little investment or commitment. I wish I could tell you how many people have come to me for counseling, miserable and absolutely desperate for change...until I told them there would be homework. We get married, expecting bliss to come as easily to us as it does to the fictitious people on the big screen. Many people even follow Jesus believing He will make their lives easier in the here and now. We love fairy tales because they enable us to be all about us.

But fairy tales don't exist. When we invest our hopes in them and they don't materialize, we can end up disillusioned and frustrated, maybe even giving up.

The next passage calls us to a simple solution--become desperate and disabused. Desperate and disabused. They don't sound like pleasant words, not nearly as grand as dreams and fairy tales. "Desperate" has almost universally negative connotations, and you might even be wondering what "disabused" means. However, these are great words when used to describe the godly picture of the Song. In our relationship with Christ and in our marriages, we must be desperate and disabused if we would know fulfillment.

The Song (3:1–11)

(She)

1 On my bed by night I sought him whom my soul loves; I sought him, but found him not.

2 I will rise now and go about the city, in the streets and in the squares; I will seek him whom my soul loves. I sought him, but found him not.

3 The watchmen found me as they went about in the city. "Have you seen him whom my soul loves?"

4 Scarcely had I passed them when I found him whom my soul loves. I held him, and would not let him go until I had brought him into my mother's house, and into the chamber of her who conceived me.

5 I adjure you, O daughters of Jerusalem, by the gazelles or the does of the field, that you not stir up or awaken love until it pleases.

6 What is that coming up from the wilderness like columns of smoke, perfumed with myrrh and frankincense, with all the fragrant powders of a merchant?

7 Behold, it is the litter of Solomon! Around it are sixty mighty men, some of the mighty men of Israel,

8 all of them wearing swords and expert in war, each with his sword at his thigh, against terror by night.

9 King Solomon made himself a carriage from the wood of Lebanon.

10 He made its posts of silver, its back of gold, its seat of purple; its interior was inlaid with love by the daughters of Jerusalem.

11 Go out, O daughters of Zion, and look upon King Solomon, with the crown with which his mother crowned him on the day of his wedding, on the day of the gladness of his heart.

In the previous passage, the man pursued the woman. Now, the woman pursues the man: "On my bed by night I sought him whom my soul loves; I sought him, but found him not" (3:1).[1] The idea is that she's looking for him in bed, but he's not there. Based upon the previous chapter, we might think, "Oh well, she'll just go back to sleep and wait for him to find her. After all, he's like a gazelle on cleft

---

[1] Some editors and commentators believe that this is a dream sequence, usually because they hold that this is not a married couple; the wedding has not happened yet. The thought is that they don't yet share a bed, so this must be a dream. In v5, she takes him to her mother's house to the very chamber where she herself was conceived, which would be highly inappropriate for an unmarried woman to do. For this reason also, they say it must be a dream.

However, as we have noted, there have been numerous places in the song where it appears that the two have been engaged in sexual relations prior to this supposed dream sequence. Therefore, a dream right here does not fix the problem. Additionally, 5:2 reads, "I slept, but my heart was awake," language that is much more conducive to being interpreted as a dream. Yet, most interpreters hold that what follows 5:2 is not a dream. It seems that some interpreters find a dream in ch3, not because the text warrants it, but because they need a dream there in order to uphold their view these are two unmarried people. If we just let the text speak and allow that they're already married, the difficulty goes away.

mountains. He's just as eager for her as she is for him." We certainly don't expect her to do what she does.

"I will rise now and go about the city, in the streets and in the squares; I will seek him whom my soul loves. I sought him, but found him not" (3:2). Women in the Ancient Near East didn't do this—leave the house in the middle of the night to go wandering about the streets in search of a man. This is dangerous, not to mention inconvenient and highly unnecessary. She knows that he desires her, as depicted in the previous passage. Plus, who wants to get out of bed in the middle of the night and go wandering about the streets looking for somebody that is eventually going to come home anyway? Some of us don't even get out of bed in the middle of the night when we smell smoke.

Yet, she is obsessed with finding him. These two verses are filled with verbs that communicate urgency and even desperation. The verb for "seek" is used four times in two verses. She's going out to do work, to spend herself, aware of the danger.

She's desperate. We tend to use the word desperate in strictly negative ways. When we say, "Oh, she's desperate," we mean, "She'll settle for anything with a pulse. She's got no standards." That's not the kind of desperation demonstrated by the woman of the Song. Rather, she's desperate in the sense that she is driven to recklessness. There is this one thing that she must have, and she's willing to do whatever is necessary to attain it. People who are desperate in this sense are fearless, determined, and willing to do dangerous things in order to get what they desire.

Think of a mother protecting her child from an abductor. She will do whatever it takes. She doesn't stop to process risk versus reward. She doesn't care. She's desperate. Love does that.

That is what we see happening in this woman in the Song. She enters a very dangerous situation, looking for her husband. And this is critical to note: it seems unwarranted. She's in no danger of losing him. *She just wants him.*

"The watchmen found me as they went about in the city. 'Have you seen him whom my soul loves?'" (3:3). What were the watchmen doing when they found her? They were going about in the city. That's the same phrase from verse 2, where she says, "I will rise now and go about the city." The watchmen of the city were like the policemen. By intentionally using the same verb for her and for them, the writer reminds us that she is doing something dangerous. She's doing something that only the watchmen should be doing—going about in the city at night. Again, all she cares about is finding him. She simply asks of them, "Have you seen him whom my soul loves?"

"Scarcely had I passed them when I found him whom my soul loves. I held him, and would not let him go until I had brought him into my mother's house, and into the chamber of her who conceived me" (3:4). That is desperation. She happens upon the police, doesn't ask them for help but for information, and when they don't have any, she abandons them and continues her mission.

When she finds her husband, she holds him, does not let him go, and brings him into her mother's house. This is exactly what we should expect. It's not that she was rescuing him from the dark. She wasn't desperate to save his life. She was desperate for *him*. Finding him, she takes him somewhere private so that they might be intimate once again. That this is another occasion for sexual intimacy is indicated by the refrain of verse 5.

"I adjure you, O daughters of Jerusalem, by the gazelles or the does of the field, that you not stir up or awaken love until it pleases" (3:5). Each time this shows up, the man and the woman are doing something that the daughters of Jerusalem should wait to do. Eventually, we'll spend a good bit of time on it, but that will come in the last chapter of the Song.

The rest of the passage serves as a contrast to what we've already seen:

What is that coming up from the wilderness like columns of smoke, perfumed with myrrh and frankincense, with all the fragrant powders of a merchant? Behold, it is the litter of Solomon! Around it are sixty mighty men, some of the mighty men of Israel, all of them wearing swords and expert in war, each with his sword at his thigh, against terror by night. King Solomon made himself a carriage from the wood of Lebanon. He made its posts of silver, its back of gold, its seat of purple; its interior was inlaid with love by the daughters of Jerusalem. Go out, O daughters of Zion, and look upon King Solomon,

with the crown with which his mother crowned him on the day
of his wedding, on the day of the gladness of his heart (3:6–11).

Remember that Solomon serves as a foil for the idealized love
depicted in the Song. This is the first of three times where he is used
to highlight something about the love of the man and woman.[2] Here,
his love in the second scene is contrasted with theirs in the first. When
we consider the scenes side-by-side, what do we find?

Look at the grandeur of the second scene compared to the
desperation of the former. There is tremendous fanfare, opulence, and
protection around this bride being brought to Solomon. She is in a
beautiful litter made of the finest materials built in Solomon's name
by other women. She is surrounded by mighty men of Israel—60 of
them, to be exact. That's twice the number of bodyguards that King
David himself had. She is perfumed with myrrh, frankincense, and all

---

[2] Some commentators split this chapter in half, taking it to be two somewhat unrelated
passages, but there are a number of things the two scenes have in common that would
indicate they are intended to be compared and contrasted.

First of all, in both scenes there is a woman coming to a man. That may not be
obvious in the second scene. Some editions entitle the second scene something like,
"He arrives for the wedding," but that does not coincide with the grammar of the
passage. V6 more literally reads, "Who is this?" "This" is a feminine singular. In other
words, "Who is this woman coming up from the wilderness like columns of smoke?"

It's a little confusing because v7 reads, "It is the litter of Solomon." It is
Solomon's litter but that doesn't mean that he's the one in it. The question being asked
is not *What is this?* but *Who is this?* A person is the answer to the question, and it must
be a feminine person. A feminine person is being brought in that litter. So some
interpreters understand this to mean that this is one of Solomon's brides being
brought to him in his litter. Therefore, similar to vv1–5, we have a woman coming to
a man.

Second, there is the phrase "by night" found in both scenes. We might not
normally make much of that phrase, but it is only used four times in the entire Hebrew
Old Testament. Two of them are in this one chapter. The bride of the Song goes out
into the danger "of the night" in v1. The soldiers surrounding Solomon's bride are
armed against terror "of the night" in v8. It seems that we're intended to compare
these two things.

Third, a mother is mentioned in both scenes. The bride brings her husband to
her mother's house, and Solomon's mother crowned him with a wedding crown.

Finally, both scenes end with a command to the daughters of Jerusalem. The
woman swears them to an oath in v5, "I adjure you...that you not stir up or awaken
love until it pleases." Those same daughters are called out to look at Solomon in v11.
There are enough things in these two passages side-by-side to indicate that they are
intended to be looked at together and compared and contrasted.

the fragrant powders of a merchant. She is literally being carried to Solomon. No exertion is required of her in the least; she is doing nothing. Solomon is wearing a crown given to him by his mother. It's all taking place in broad daylight with the admiration of all the daughters of Jerusalem.

Contrast this with the seeming indignity of the former scene. The bride of the Song risks her own life, completely unprotected against the night. She has no help even from the police. There is no fanfare, and no one even knows what she is doing. She's not being carried, but she wears herself out finding her husband. There are no opulent accommodations. Rather, she takes her husband back to her mother's house! She's a desperate woman. Yet, she evidently enjoys a passion that moves her to once again exhort the daughters of Jerusalem to chastity until they are married, "This is so wonderful—it's well worth the wait."

Solomon is living a fairy tale, but the shepherdess has real-life satisfaction. It will become clearer each time Solomon appears in the Song that what this husband and wife have is preferable to what he has.[3] The woman in the litter may be enjoying some pomp and fanfare, but she is simply going to join 999 other wives in his harem. She's riding in a nice car, being treated like a princess for a day, but she will never know the joy known by the shepherdess of this Song. The early part of chapter 3 shows the wife exhibiting a desperate,

---

[3] These scenes are setting us up for several later scenes in the Song. In ch5, the woman cannot be bothered to get out of bed even to unlock the door for her husband. She suffers tremendously for this. That later scene tends to highlight the virtue of what she does here, which is to tirelessly pursue her husband and then enjoy him. Her desperation shown here is virtuous.

We also find in ch8 a contrast between Solomon's vineyard and the woman's vineyard. Solomon has this enormous vineyard—his harem—cared for by others. The woman of the Song has her vineyard, which is her one husband. She essentially says to Solomon, "You can have your extravagant vineyard; I want mine. What I have—hard-won, monogamous love—is preferable to what you have." That's a huge clue to what's going on here in ch3.

There's also a scene in ch6 where she is shown as the husband's one unique, special wife contrasted with the many, indistinct queens and concubines of Solomon. Again, the idea is that what the man and woman have is preferable to what Solomon has. Solomon, whom I hold to be the author of this Song, does not expect us to forget about the reality of his love life. He had many, many wives. He never knew the closeness of monogamous love depicted in the marriage of the man and woman.

exhausting pursuit of intimacy. The latter part of the chapter looks very much like a fairytale, what everyone would want. Yet, we will find later in the Song that the relationship for which the most energy is expended is the one worth having. The fairy tale leads to meaninglessness.

The woman of the Song is not only desperate, but disabused. To disabuse is to open someone's eyes to a false belief or a superstition. "Go out...and look upon King Solomon," the woman says in verse 11. She's preparing the daughters of Zion to see later on that the fairy tale leads to something other than what she has, and that what she has is truly desirable.

The path that everyone would want in marriage—pageantry, ease, wealth, zero adversity—is not only a path that simply does not exist in the real world, but if banked upon, will never end in a place of fulfillment. You will only find heartache. True joy and fulfillment in marriage come at the end of the road paved with hard work and good, godly desperation.

Desperate, Disabused Discipleship

Anyone who pursues fellowship with Jesus as we have considered in the previous chapters will likely experience a growing desire for Him. Yet, few reach the level of desperation for Christ exhibited by the bride in the Song. Why is this? One cannot become desperate until he or she is disabused of wrong thinking about the Christian life. Some believers have fallen prey to teaching that portrays Jesus as the path to easy street. Jesus is presented as the answer to all of life's troubles. Some charlatans even go so far as to preach that if you follow Jesus, having enough faith, you'll never get sick, never be poor, and never suffer. Such things simply cannot be reconciled with the New Testament, and we must be disabused of them. If we aren't, we will value Jesus for what He gives us rather than for who He is, and when He doesn't deliver the fairy tale He may be discarded.

Here is the preeminent truth that must displace the notion that Jesus leads to easy street: Jesus calls us to suffering...and He is so magnificent and glorious that in His service such things are not only worthwhile, but ultimately fulfilling. To become desperate and disabused, we must recognize four parts to this truth.

Discipleship is a life of suffering. Peter wrote to the believers of Asia Minor, "Beloved, do not be surprised at the fiery trial when it comes upon you to test you, as though something strange were happening to you. But rejoice insofar as you share Christ's sufferings, that you may also rejoice and be glad when his glory is revealed" (1 Pet. 4:12–13). It is not a strange thing for a Christian to suffer. Rather, it would be strange for a Christian not to suffer. Paul went a step further, characterizing suffering as a gift: "For it has been granted to you that for the sake of Christ you should not only believe in him but also suffer for his sake" (Phil. 1:29). What an explosive verse! Suffering is every bit as much a gift as faith!

Suffering blesses us in several ways. First, by suffering we are able to participate in the Lord's work of spreading the gospel.[4] Second, by suffering we are better able to comfort others who suffer in similar ways.[5] Third, and most gloriously, by suffering we experience more of His power and grace.[6] This is precisely why it is good and, consequently, good for us. The mature, desperate believer doesn't run from suffering, but embraces it as an old friend who makes Jesus sweeter.

Discipleship is a life of hard work. As we saw in the last passage, Jesus pursues us for fellowship as the man pursues the woman in the Song. Jesus has gone to great lengths to make a way for us to have a relationship with him, leaving his eternal throne, taking on humanity, bearing our sins in his body on the tree, dying under the wrath of God, being raised by the Father for our justification, ascending to the right hand, sending His Spirit to live inside of us, and now ever living to intercede for us. While we rightly believe that all the blessings of salvation are a gift purchased by the blood of Jesus, it is still the case that the enjoyment of these blessings in the present life requires a constant, volitional struggle on our part. The New Testament uses words like "strive," "struggle," and "make every effort" to describe the energy with which we are to pursue the

---

[4] Acts 5:40–41; Col. 1:24–26; 1 Pet. 2:12–25

[5] 2 Cor. 1:3–10, 7:5–7

[6] 2 Cor. 4:8–10, 12:3–10; Phil. 3:8–11, 4:11–13

Christian life.[7] "Put to death the deeds of the body…consider yourself dead to sin…submit your members as instruments of righteousness to God…pray without ceasing…flee from lust, and pursue righteousness."[8] Growth in godliness, as pursued by putting off sin and putting on righteousness, is some of the hardest work we will ever do. It is also the most pleasurable in that it makes us more like Jesus.

Discipleship is a life of warfare. Paul repeatedly likens disciples to soldiers.[9] A believer's life is one of spiritual warfare against an intelligent enemy bent on deceiving and devouring us.[10] It is no life of temporal ease and safety, but one of fighting, killing, running, exerting, trusting, and pouring oneself out in pursuit of the One loved.[11] Certainly, our warfare is against the god of this world, but we also have to contend with our own flesh—incompletely sanctified hearts that are prone to stray.[12] Therefore, there is a constant battle for our own affections, requiring daily, hourly, even minute-by-minute warfare against our flesh—an ever increasing vigilance against our own appetite for idolatry.[13] We must fight to become indifferent to the things that do not lead us toward Christ and to hate the things that lead us away from Him. Left alone, our affections will go anywhere but after Him. We need constant reminders of the gospel and a tireless impulse for turning to Him in everything and for everything. We must live with the realization that we simply cannot know Him and enjoy Him fully without standing shoulder to shoulder—on our knees— with other soldiers in the fight.[14]

The apostle teaches that this demands a particular mindset—a wartime mentality: "No soldier gets entangled in civilian pursuits, since his aim is to please the one who enlisted him" (2 Tim. 2:4). War

---

[7] Luke 13:24; Rom. 15:30; 1 Cor. 14:12; Phil. 1:27; Col. 1:29, 4:12; 1 Tim. 4:10; Heb. 4:11, 12:4, 12:14; 2 Pet. 1:5

[8] Rom. 6:11, 6:13, 8:13; Col. 3:5; 1 Thess. 5:17; 2 Tim. 2:22

[9] Phil. 2:25; 2 Tim. 2:3–4; Phm. 1:2

[10] Eph. 6:10–18; 2 Cor. 11:3; 1 Pet. 5:8

[11] Col. 3:5; 1 Cor. 9:24–26; 2 Cor. 10:3–4; Gal. 2:2, 5:7; Phil. 2:17; 1 Tim. 6:12; 2 Tim. 4:6–7; Heb. 12:1

[12] Gal. 5:16–17

[13] Pro. 4:23; 1 Cor. 10:14; Jas. 1:14; 1 John 5:21

[14] Acts 4:23–31; Rom. 15:30–32; 2 Cor. 1:11; Eph. 6:18–20; Col. 4:12; 1 Thess. 5:25; Jas. 5:13–18

demands single-minded focus. Our lives must be about the battle, not comparatively meaningless, temporal interests. The disciple's life is all Jesus all the time. There is no second-tier, non-combatant kind of discipleship.

Jesus makes all these things sweet. All the above sounds like a whole lot of effort. It is. That's why Jesus said to "count the cost" (Luke 14:28). "The gate is narrow and the way is hard that leads to life, and those who find it are few" (Matt. 7:14). Yet, for those whose eyes have been opened by the Holy Spirit to see the beauty of Christ—just like the woman in the Song—we see the cost and we don't care. The woman in the Song is desperate because she loves the man. She's not in love with running around in the dark at night, nor is she in any real danger of losing him. She just wants to be with him *right now*. To the extent that we feel that way about Jesus we will suffer, work, and fight with great delight, understanding that the whole thing is about a person, not simply inheriting a location after we die. Again, "This is eternal life, that they know you the only true God, and Jesus Christ whom you have sent" (John 17:3). Let us pray that we would be desperate for Him and disabused of the notion that the Christian life is easy.

Embracing A Wonderful Reality

If marriage is a picture of the relationship of Christ and the church, we can commend the desirability of Christ by tirelessly pursuing a godly marriage. Just as union with Christ holds great joy, so also there is something wonderful to be had in the union of a husband and wife. And just as discipleship entails a life of suffering and hard work, so also the bliss of human marriage does not come easily. Accordingly, we must count the cost and give ourselves completely to its pursuit, knowing that it is worth the effort. Christian marriage is intended to tell that story about the gospel.

Yet, the worldly fairy tale of love would say that you're going to find someone who is perfectly compatible with you, will fit you like a glove, make you blissfully happy, won't hurt you, will make right all your past problems, heartaches, and family trauma, and will offer ongoing romantic and erotic love. In fact, your love will be so special that nothing in the world will be able to threaten it. It will be stronger than any problem you could ever face. The struggle is over. You're whole now. You're going to live happily ever after.

Storybooks, love songs, and movies sell this, and our self-centered hearts continue to buy it even after we get married and it doesn't materialize for us personally. Some of us convince ourselves that the fairy tale still exists, just not with the person that we married.

We need to wake up. The struggle isn't over when we get married. The struggle begins...for something wonderful. The love for which marriage is built does exist, but it comes as a result of selfless, reckless abandon. The fairy tale is a tool of the devil intended to cause dissatisfaction with God's good gift of marriage. We want the fairy tale that delivers easy, pain-free joy—a kind of marriage that simply does not exist. The devil knows that as long as we hold onto that fairy tale, we will never experience the joy that God actually intends to eventuate from a godly, desperate marriage.

This passage calls us to be disabused of the devil's fairy tale and become inflamed with the desperation of the woman of the Song. If we're going to know the bliss of marital intimacy, we cannot wait for it to come to us like a painted bride on an opulent marriage litter. That's a pipe-dream. We must chase it down in the night like a frantic, half-crazed lover. That's reality.

We have to do the hard work. Remember that the Fall has rendered both you and your spouse self-centered power-mongers. Even the quietest of people have within their hearts the desire to do their own thing and have their own way. The good news is that the gospel has given all the tools necessary to live a pre-Fall marriage. However, because we have incompletely sanctified hearts, it takes work. Hard work. Therefore, we must embrace the hard work, tenaciously fighting for the godly love that God has designed for us.

Hard work will mean different things in different marriages. You may have years of hurts that have piled up. The thought of working through them is beyond daunting, like an insurmountable mountain. Look to Christ and the hill He climbed to make you His. No one has ever worked harder or endured more pain than the Lord Jesus. Honor and commend Him by vowing you'll die before you give up.

On the other hand, your problems may not seem that serious. However, even garden variety issues do not get resolved without determination to do so. If you're a bad communicator, own it, and work on it. If your spouse says you're insensitive, you probably are. Recognize it and ask a brother or sister in Christ, perhaps even a pastor, to help you. Approach this like you would with any gift in your life that requires regular maintenance. Determine what needs to be done and get after it!

We have to say yes to counseling. For some, going to counseling is the highest admission of personal failure and defeat, so pride keeps them away. For others, the pain of the past is bad enough without a stranger entering the mix. Still others refuse because they believe the problems in the marriage exist only in the head of their spouse. Godly desperation will move you to say yes to counseling even if you don't think you need it. When your spouse asks you to go to counseling, you have just been told your spouse is distressed. If you say no, you may have just communicated, "I don't care; you're not worth the trouble." Such a sentiment is wholly unacceptable for those who would emulate Christ.

Get up and run after your spouse! Stop waiting for someone else to feed you happiness. Do the godly thing and chase your spouse into the counseling room! Show some godly desperation. Let the *counselor* decide whether or not you need counseling.

We have to say no to self. What is personally convenient just happens to be what is often deadly for intimacy. Search the Gospels. You'll never find on the lips of Jesus the idea, "I just don't feel like it" or "That's not good for me." A Christ interested strictly in His own pleasure never would have left heaven. There was nothing convenient about His condescension, incarnation, temptation, and crucifixion. There was nothing easy about pouring Himself out for His bride. However, that's what godly love does. It pours itself out. Jesus emptied Himself. If we would commend His gospel in our marriages, we must also empty ourselves in our desperate pursuit of the one we love.

There are any number of ways this could be applied depending upon your unique situation. If non-essential things—hobbies, career, etc.—are preventing you from spending quality time with your spouse, get ruthless with your own calendar and self-interest. Remove whatever needs to be removed in order to make time for what is truly important—your spouse. If your parents have put themselves between you and your spouse, take it upon yourself to address the situation with them. Confess sin and ask forgiveness. Embrace the inconvenient and seemingly unnecessary.

The woman on Solomon's litter ends up with nothing special. She's just another body enjoyed by Solomon. That's the picture of the person married today who is content either to wait for the fairy tale or to live with disillusionment and resentment over unmet expectations. The woman of the Song who chases down her husband at night enjoys a truly unique and passionate love that a precious few know in this life—a precious few who refuse to be held back from bliss by the apparent indignity of showing godly desperation. Which will you be?

You may not want to let go of the fairy tale. The truth is the fairy tale is poisonous. It will cause you to resent your spouse. That fairy tale was not a gift from God. Your spouse is a gift from God. He has designed for the goodness of marriage to be received through the strenuous pursuit of intimacy. Our being disabused of the fairy tale should lead us not to sadness, but to glad freedom. We are no longer deceived, and we're free to passionately chase what God has given us.

Discussion Questions/Activities

1. Have you ever come under teaching that portrayed Christianity as the doorway to an easy life, or perhaps, prosperity, health, and happiness? How has your life demonstrated this teaching to be false?

2. How would you characterize your pursuit of Christ? Desperate and disabused, or apathetic and deceived? What specific changes can you make to treat your walk with the Lord as a desperate pursuit?

3. In what ways have you been "riding the litter"—expecting happiness to just happen rather than working for it with godly desperation? Discuss these things with your spouse. In what specific ways can you begin to work hard to pursue a godly marriage?

4. Do you and your spouse have issues you have tried to work through on your own, but without positive change? List those

issues with your spouse. Given the teaching of this chapter, what *good* reason can you give for not pursuing counseling?

5. Has your spouse asked you to go to counseling in the past, but you refused? If so, seek his/her forgiveness and make an appointment with your pastor to talk about counseling before you read the next chapter.

CRESCENDO & CULMINATION

Spoiled

Confession: I'm a recovering Star Wars nerd. The George Lucas prequels and subsequent Disney abominations have aided my recovery. However, there was a time when I cared deeply about these movies. The first prequel was a dud, but I assumed everyone has a misfire at some point. So when the second prequel was in post-production, I was very eager to see it. Yet, I wanted to try something I'd never done before by attempting to be completely surprised by the details of the movie. Essentially, I wanted to walk into that theater as a proverbial blank slate—no idea what was going to happen. *I wanted the raw experience.*

This was no small task given that Star Wars nerds can talk about little else during the buildup to a new movie. With tremendous dedication and mental energy, I fled all casual conversations related to the film itself or the franchise. Additionally, I intentionally stayed away from previews, articles, and interviews about the movie. There were many, many close calls.

All this effort to achieve a blank slate created intense anticipation of this movie for me. The months leading up to the release of the film were like the opening lines of a Pavarotti performance--latent energy promising to crescendo and culminate in a mesmerizing experience. With each passing week in which I avoided learning anything about the movie, the expectation of pleasure grew. "I might just pull this off! It's going to be wonderful!" I even surmised, "This has to be a first in Star Wars fandom…"

The crescendo of anticipation grew until the day of culmination. As I arrived with my wife and young son at the theater, I thought, "I've done it. I've achieved blank-slateness. Culmination awaits." Only a fool would work that hard for such a glorious payoff only to ruin it by taking a bathroom break in the middle of the movie, so I visited the restroom before it started.

An evil, evil man in the restroom asked me, "You seeing Star Wars?" Before I could think to plug my ears and flee, I responded in the affirmative. My heart stopped and the world moved in slow motion as he robbed me of cinematic joy by uttering three words: "Yoda comes unglued."[1]

I was numb. This villain spoiled what was, in my opinion, the only great moment of the film. Months of crescendo. No culmination.

The human heart is built for crescendo and culmination. The escalating pain of a woman in labor can only be rightly answered by the cry of a newborn baby. The slow chink-chink-chink climb to the top of a roller coaster creates anticipation that can only be fulfilled by the roaring drop down the first hill. We are wired to feel tension and to expect that tension to build to something spectacular. We want it in our entertainment, we expect it in our lives, and we even interpret history in terms of crescendo and culmination. The human heart desires culmination. It is foreign, unnatural, and—as we'll see in the next section of the Song—even ungodly to have crescendo without culmination.

The Song (4:1–5:1)

(He)

1 Behold, you are beautiful, my love, behold, you are beautiful! Your eyes are doves behind your veil. Your hair is like a flock of goats leaping down the slopes of Gilead.

---

[1] It is not lost on me that I've just lamented a spoiler by committing one. However, since the movie in question is over 17 years old, there are likely not many people who would care. For this reason, I felt safe in my apparent hypocrisy.

2 Your teeth are like a flock of shorn ewes that have come up from the washing, all of which bear twins, and not one among them has lost its young.

3 Your lips are like a scarlet thread, and your mouth is lovely. Your cheeks are like halves of a pomegranate behind your veil.

4 Your neck is like the tower of David, built in rows of stone; on it hang a thousand shields, all of them shields of warriors.

5 Your two breasts are like two fawns, twins of a gazelle, that graze among the lilies.

6 Until the day breathes and the shadows flee, I will go away to the mountain of myrrh and the hill of frankincense.

7 You are altogether beautiful, my love; there is no flaw in you.

8 Come with me from Lebanon, my bride; come with me from Lebanon. Depart from the peak of Amana, from the peak of Senir and Hermon, from the dens of lions, from the mountains of leopards.

9 You have captivated my heart, my sister, my bride; you have captivated my heart with one glance of your eyes, with one jewel of your necklace.

10 How beautiful is your love, my sister, my bride! How much better is your love than wine, and the fragrance of your oils than any spice!

11 Your lips drip nectar, my bride; honey and milk are under your tongue; the fragrance of your garments is like the fragrance of Lebanon.

12 A garden locked is my sister, my bride, a spring locked, a fountain sealed.

13 Your shoots are an orchard of pomegranates with all choicest fruits, henna with nard,

14 nard and saffron, calamus and cinnamon, with all trees of frankincense, myrrh and aloes, with all choice spices--

15 a garden fountain, a well of living water, and flowing streams from Lebanon.

16a Awake, O north wind, and come, O south wind! Blow upon my garden, let its spices flow.

(She)
16b Let my beloved come to his garden, and eat its choicest fruits.

(He)
1a I came to my garden, my sister, my bride, I gathered my myrrh with my spice, I ate my honeycomb with my honey, I drank my wine with my milk.

(Chorus)
1b Eat, friends, drink, and be drunk with love!

The entire passage represents crescendo that culminates in 5:1, the exact middle of the Song. The husband, who does almost all the speaking in this passage, begins the crescendo by praising his wife's beauty:

> Behold, you are beautiful, my love, behold, you are beautiful! Your eyes are doves behind your veil. Your hair is like a flock of goats leaping down the slopes of Gilead. Your teeth are like a flock of shorn ewes that have come up from the washing, all of which bear twins, and not one among them has lost its young. Your lips are like a scarlet thread, and your mouth is lovely. Your cheeks are like halves of a pomegranate behind your veil. Your neck is like the tower of David, built in rows of stone; on it hang a thousand shields, all of them shields of warriors. Your two breasts are like two fawns, twins of a gazelle, that graze among the lilies (4:1-5).

This is not exactly how we would sweet-talk a spouse in the modern West. We tend to be a bit more literal in our compliments; therefore, our minds want to read this text very literally. However, we must read these words with the original culture in mind. These things that sound so peculiar to us would have been quite flattering to her. Even without an ancient Hebrew metaphor decoder ring, we can know what the husband intends to communicate.[2] Verses 1 and 7

---

2 Commentaries differ widely on the proper understanding of each individual metaphor. For this reason and for the sake of brevity, I have chosen not to deal with each one separately. Their collective meaning is clear from the context.

interpret the metaphors for us. When he looks at her, he sees beauty. He says so three times—twice in verse 1 and once in verse 7: "Behold, you are beautiful, my love, behold, you are beautiful...You are altogether beautiful, my love; there is no flaw in you." These verses are like bookends making sense of the metaphors in between. He's telling her she is beautiful.

But, looking leads somewhere. It builds. Verse 6 reads, "Until the day breathes and the shadows flee, I will go away to the mountain of myrrh and the hill of frankincense." It doesn't take a seminary degree to interpret verse 6, especially when it follows immediately after verse 5, which reads, "Your two breasts are like two fawns, twins of a gazelle, that graze among the lilies." When he looks at her, he sees beauty, but it does not stop there. Looking crescendos to desire. He wants her. Take the time to review the first few chapters of the Song and you'll see this isn't the first time this has happened; it's just the most detailed.

We might wonder, "Is she beautiful because he loves her, or does he love her because she's beautiful?" The context suggests the former. She is beautiful because he loves her. He says, "There is no flaw in you," and yet we know she's flawed. She has been baked in the sun. Nobody wants the tan girl in the Ancient Near East. Is he lying when he calls her flawless? No, this is what he sees. He loves her, so when he looks at her, he sees beauty. Saying that love is blind is not the best way to communicate what is happening here. It's preferable to say beauty is in the eye of the beholder. She may be unattractive by conventional standards, but just try convincing him of that. When he looks at her, he really sees the definition of beauty...because he loves her.

In verse 8, there is further crescendo as he calls her to come with him: "Come with me from Lebanon, my bride; come with me from Lebanon. Depart from the peak of Amana, from the peak of Senir and Hermon, from the dens of lions, from the mountains of leopards." Each of these peaks represent desolate, dangerous places. He's saying, "Come with me away from those places to a place of lush safety." Looking has progressed to desire which has led to an invitation. The energy of the passage is building. "You're flawless...I desire you...come with me."

Beginning in verses 9 and 10, he extols her captivating loving: "You have captivated my heart, my sister, my bride; you have captivated my heart with one glance of your eyes, with one jewel of your necklace. How beautiful is your love, my sister, my bride! How much better is your love than wine, and the fragrance of your oils than any spice!"[3]

Verse 9 is at the center of the passage. Its statement— "You have captivated my heart"—is a way of saying, "I'm yours and yours only. I don't just think you're wonderful and I don't just want you, but I belong to you."

There are a couple of things to note about verse 10, "How beautiful is your love, my sister, my bride! How much better is your love than wine, and the fragrance of your oils than any spice!" First, he is not talking merely about her love, that is, her capacity to have affection. The text more literally reads, "How beautiful is your loving, how much better is your loving than wine." This is a comment about her sexual acts of love, which indicates that he has experienced them.[4]

Second, he describes her in the same way she described him in the beginning of the Song. Remember that she spoke of him in exalted terms, but herself in very understated terms. He was magnificent, but she was common. Now she is described the same way that he was described. It's possible we are intended to see that she is becoming like him. At the very least, we are intended to understand that he sees her that way. He finds her loving delightful.

The crescendo continues in verses 11–16:

Your lips drip nectar, my bride; honey and milk are under your tongue; the fragrance of your garments is like the fragrance of Lebanon. A garden locked is my sister, my bride, a spring locked, a fountain sealed. Your shoots are an orchard of

---

[3] Why "sister"? As I studied the Song in preparation to preach it, I playfully began to use some of the pet names found there with my wife. She invited me to stop using "sister." It sounds odd to our modern ears, but "sister" was a common term of endearment from husbands to wives in that culture. It would have been very natural to the original reader.

[4] Here we find yet another reason to understand these two to be a married couple. With the more traditional reading, they are wooing each other just before their wedding night. Such a reading simply does not account for this language, much less the numerous similar passages already encountered by this point in the Song.

pomegranates with all choicest fruits, henna with nard, nard and saffron, calamus and cinnamon, with all trees of frankincense, myrrh and aloes, with all choice spices—a garden fountain, a well of living water, and flowing streams from Lebanon. Awake, O north wind, and come, O south wind! Blow upon my garden, let its spices flow.

Her loving is described in the most desirable terms possible. Notice that he calls her a garden locked, a spring locked, a fountain sealed. Some commentators, because of their presupposition that the man and woman are not yet married, understand these phrases to mean she is a virgin who has saved herself for him. That does not fit the larger context. Even within this passage, he makes comments about parts of her body that only someone with access to the garden would be able to make.

It is more likely that she is a garden locked in the sense that she belongs only to him, a metaphorical answer to his confession that she has captivated his heart. Each belongs only to the other. Remember that Solomon has written this, using himself numerous times as a foil for the love shared between the woman and the man. He is making much of the monogamy of their love. She's a garden of choice fruit that only her husband has tasted. She's a well of living water that only her husband has enjoyed. These verses represent her husband celebrating the fact that he alone knows her this way.

The celebration of that exclusive intimacy serves to ramp up the expectation of where this is heading as he calls on the wind to stir her up. It's all crescendo leading to an obvious culmination. Consider how odd it would be for the Song to simply stop right there—for him to say all these highly charged lines, building to 16a, a better translation of which would be: "*Arouse*, north wind; come in south wind! Blow on my garden, let its spices flow!" Given that the passage is clear that the garden is her body, this is a not-so-veiled call for her to be sexually aroused. How unnatural then for these two to shake hands and say, "Well, good night." This scene wants to go somewhere obvious…and it does.

With verse 16b, the wife says: "Let my beloved come to his garden, and eat its choicest fruits." In 5:1, he accepts: "I came to my garden, my sister, my bride, I gathered my myrrh with my spice, I ate my honeycomb with my honey, I drank my wine with my milk." The chorus cheers them on: "Eat, friends, drink, and be drunk with love!"

There are other heightened scenes in the Song, but this is the highest. Culmination. Intimacy is where the whole passage naturally wants to go. There is a natural crescendo from beauty to attraction to delightful captivity to intimacy. He has loved her. He sees her beauty. He is captivated by her. He expresses these things to her. Intimacy is the natural expression. Crescendo and culmination.

We can crystalize three truths from this portion of the Song. **First, marital love, as God intended, sees beauty in the one loved.** He loves her, so he sees beauty in every part of her. **Second, marital love, as God intended, is potently monogamous.** He is captivated. She is a garden locked. The word "mine" is used nine times in the original text of 5:1 alone. **Third, marital love, as God intended, is expressed in passionate intimacy.** For the scene to stop short of passionate intimacy would be wholly unnatural and bizarre.

The Consummation of All Things

Just as there was a clear trajectory toward intimate fulfillment in this scene of the Song, so also the gospel creates in us great anticipation of closeness with Christ. Jesus Himself drives this crescendo toward culmination. **First, Jesus sees beauty in the one loved.** There is a theological problem with believing that God has loved us because we are beautiful. On the other hand, the Word does teach that we are beautiful because He has loved us.[5]

When the Father set His love on us from eternity past, we had no redeeming qualities. When Jesus laid down his life to save us from the wrath we so richly deserved, we had nothing to commend us to His heart. As we see so clearly in Deuteronomy 7, He loved us not because of anything in us, but simply because He loved us.[6]

---

[5] Isa. 60:15, 62:1–5; Zec. 9:16; Eph. 1:4, 5:25–27; 1Thess. 5:23; Heb. 12:22–24; Rev. 21:2

[6] Deut. 7:7–8: "It was not because you were more in number than any other people that the LORD set his love on you and chose you, for you were the fewest of all peoples, but it is because the LORD loves you and is keeping the oath that he swore to your fathers, that the LORD has brought you out with a mighty hand and redeemed you from the house of slavery, from the hand of Pharaoh king of Egypt."

We were unlovely when He set His love on us, but His work on the cross has not left us that way. Through the cross and resurrection, Jesus removed our stain of sin and our guilt, and He has imputed to us His righteousness. In the sight of God, we wear the righteousness of the eternal, beloved Jesus. We are lovely because we are in Christ. Just as the woman is described in the same terms as the husband here in chapter 4, so have we been declared righteous because of the righteousness of Jesus credited to us by faith.

What isn't clear at this point in the Song is whether the woman is actually changing, or if she is just viewed as flawless by her husband. Is her love truly better than wine? Or is he just blinded by love? It's not obvious in chapter 4, but later in the Song others will praise her exceptional beauty. You see, it's not just that his love has changed the way he sees her, but his love has actually changed her.

Similarly, we have been declared righteous by the Father, but He is also making us righteous as we grow into the likeness of Jesus in our character and conduct. We'll spend more time on that concept when we get to chapter 6 of the Song. For now, it's worth noting that Jesus has loved us and therefore finds us beautiful. His love has caused Him to see beauty in us. We should hear the heart of Christ in the words of 4:9: "You have captivated my heart, my sister, my bride; you have captivated my heart with one glance of your eyes…" This is simply how the Lord feels about His people. The Song is not alone in the use of this kind of language. Passages like Isaiah 62 attribute similar words directly to God: "You shall no more be termed Forsaken, and your land shall no more be termed Desolate, but you shall be called My Delight Is in Her, and your land Married; for the LORD delights in you, and your land shall be married. For as a young man marries a young woman, so shall your sons marry you, and as the bridegroom rejoices over the bride, so shall your God rejoice over you" (Isa. 62:4-5). Jesus sees beauty in the one loved.

Second, Jesus desires pure monogamy with His bride. He no more wants to view our beauty from a distance without close fellowship than the man of the Song wants just to look at his wife. But what does monogamy mean in the context of our relationship with Jesus? *It means that Jesus has given Himself only to His bride.* That is, Jesus belongs exclusively to those who repent of their sin and trust in Him.

One of the great horrors of universalism is that, in a sense, it makes Jesus Himself out to be a player who gives Himself to everyone with no regard for a marriage covenant. Yet, there has been a great marriage called the New Covenant. The only partakers of that covenant are those who repent and trust in Jesus. He has given Himself only to His bride.

Jesus also naturally desires to have His bride all to Himself. He will not share us with false gods. Christ must be the sole object of our worship, our one Lord. The Old Testament pictures of Yahweh as a jealous husband and Israel as an adulteress should inform our understanding of our covenant with Jesus. Jesus as the Bridegroom desires exclusive adoration from His bride. Accordingly, we should desire to be a completely devoted and faithful spouse to the Bridegroom. It should grieve us to ever think that we might be described as having adulterous hearts.

Third, Jesus enjoys passionate intimacy with His bride. Consider salvation history in terms of crescendo and culmination. Ultimately, where does the gospel lead? The promises, hopes, types, and shadows of the Old Testament gave man a glimpse of the beauty of God and created a yearning to be restored to Him. That yearning is answered by the coming of Christ, which was foretold from the earliest parts of the Bible. Yet, His first coming was not the ultimate goal of the gospel. His first coming provided for the culmination but was not itself the culmination. No, even as Christ ascended to heaven, His followers were left anticipating something more—His return. There is a reason that theologians refer to the Second Coming as the consummation of all things. Christ's return is the ultimate end of all God's creative and salvific acts. In other words, the saving work of God in Christ finds its culmination in passionate, eternal fellowship with Him. To stop short of this is wholly unnatural.

When we conceive of the blessing of salvation as consisting solely in the elimination of wrath, we miss the sweetness of our covenant marriage with Jesus. Some believers think of their salvation as a "get out of hell free card," and then they busy themselves giving that same card to as many people as possible. Certainly, Christ's work spares us from the wrath to come, and certainly, fear of the wrath to come is a biblical motivation to flee to Christ. Yet, that is just the point—we are to flee from wrath *to Christ, a person.* We should conceive of our own salvation as being joined to Christ and having a share in Him. Evangelism is gathering others to be joined to Him, to worship Him, and to enjoy Him forever.

Imagine if I had a literal marriage that I held merely to be an escape from singleness, not an intimate relationship. How would that affect the way that I talked about my marriage and my wife? "I'm not single anymore. Isn't that great? I owe it all to my spouse. She rescued me from singleness." I might talk about her and tell other people how wonderful she is, but I would only be able to speak of her usefulness to me. I wouldn't really know her and enjoy her so as to extol her as a person. If marriage were only about escaping singleness, there would be no wedding night or ongoing sexual relationship. There would be no emotional connection, conversation, or spiritual sharing. There would only be my constant, yet impersonal talk about this person who rescued me from singleness.

Can you imagine such a thing? In that scenario, "I'm married," wouldn't mean, "I have a one-flesh relationship with this person who has captivated my heart and with whom I revel in constant monogamous intimacy." Rather, "I'm married," would just mean, "I'm not single."

That absurd picture of marriage is exactly what some people live out in their relationship with Jesus. He simply represents an escape from hell. There is no relationship, no intimacy, and no fellowship. There is no constant enjoyment of a person. In other words, there is the unnatural termination of the crescendo of the gospel, a gospel which is designed to culminate in fellowship.

I'm convinced that the reason so many people find the Christian life to be so difficult, so unmanageable, so unfulfilling, and so devoid of joy is that they have a truncated view of the trajectory of the gospel. They live as if John 17:3 reads, "And this is eternal life—no hell," rather than, "And this is eternal life, that they know you, the only true God, and Jesus Christ whom you have sent." The culmination of the gospel is not mere freedom from hell. It's eternal fellowship with the Godhead. The former was accomplished as a means to the latter. Oh, that we would well receive Christ's loving overtures and meet Him in this beautiful, monogamous intimacy, eagerly anticipating his return!

I Only Have Eyes for You

Let's be reminded that because the Lord Jesus exemplifies the love of the Song, and because our marriages are to be pictures of the gospel, we must emulate Christ's exemplary love toward our spouses. This alone is the road to our knowledge of all that God created marriage to be. So how do we emulate Christ in these things? By exhibiting a disposition toward and enjoyment of our spouses that says, "I only have eyes for you."

First, we must see beauty in the one loved. The word "see" is intentional. By it, we do not mean "look for." Some married people might testify, "There is no magic in our marriage. There's no desire. There's very little passion because my spouse is not attractive to me." Implied is that love comes from perceived inherent beauty.

However, if we look to the gospel we find that is not the case. When we recognize God as the premier authority on love, we realize what a mistake it is to expect our spouse to be a certain thing before we love them. God's elective love demonstrates that love is a decision. The Scriptures are explicit that when God set His love on us from eternity past, it had nothing to do with anything he saw in us.[7] He decided to love us. *Then* He performed incredible acts of grace and love. The result of *His* work was that we became lovely in His eyes.

We should love like that. Here lies the critical truth missing in the thinking of many. Those who repent and trust in Christ enjoy the indwelling of His Holy Spirit. If you are in Christ, the God who called all things into existence with a word lives inside of you. He exists in you, not as a sentimental gesture and not as a symbolic presence, but as power for living. Ephesians 1:18-19 tells us that immeasurable power—the very power that raised Christ from the dead—is at work in those who believe. The Lord Jesus Christ empowers the life that He commands.

By myself, I can do nothing. By the indwelling Spirit, I can do all that He calls me to do, including loving my spouse as Christ loves the church. I must decide to love my spouse. It's an act of the will. Then I must perform acts of love for my spouse, trusting in His power.

---

[7] Deut. 7:7-8, 10:15; Job 7:17; Mal. 1:2-3; Rom. 5:8, 9:10-12, 11:5-6; Eph. 2:1-9; 2 Tim. 1:9; Tit. 3:3-7

It is impossible to perform loving acts for someone via Holy Spirit power without genuine affection then growing in your heart. The perception of beauty and the growth of affection results from a decision to love. That perception of beauty comes not so much by any change in the one loved, but by our becoming like Christ in the way that we love them.

If we would commend the gospel to the world, we must stop waiting for our spouses to stir something up in us by their outward or inward beauty. We must commit to loving them well. This principle is demonstrated in Jesus' prayer in John 17. The Lord gave Himself to loving the twelve so fully that He desired not only to return to glory with the Father, but to share that glory with them. Likewise, our faithful investment of acts of love in our spouses will result in genuine affection and our seeing beauty in them.

The admonition to see beauty in the one loved really means choosing to love your spouse without regard for what your spouse evokes in you, allowing the Lord to transform the way you see your spouse. See beauty in the one loved by loving well.

Second, we must be potently monogamous. This means more than simply not having relations with other people. Some couples have never committed physical adultery, but they are in the regular habit of entertaining things like celebrity crushes, even if only playfully. Others have elaborate private fantasy lives that do not involve their spouses. Given how the Lord takes adultery to the realm of the heart, in Matthew 5:27-28, we shouldn't consider such practices indicative of true monogamy. It certainly isn't the kind of monogamy that is potent.

Potent monogamy is where I reserve myself—mentally, emotionally, physically—for one person. I don't allow fleeting thoughts of what it would be like to be even in an emotional relationship with someone else. My mind, my heart, and my body belong to my spouse. My spouse alone is the object of my romantic and sexual thoughts, affections, and actions.

This, too, is a choice. You can choose to reserve yourself—not just physically, but also emotionally and mentally—for your spouse alone. When you both do that in conjunction with the decision to love well, it creates an atmosphere of unparalleled romantic and sexual passion and fulfillment.

This is a message desperately needed by all believers in this sex-saturated culture. The world sells the lie that you cannot be fulfilled by only knowing one person. It actively advocates multiple partners before you get married. It justifies adultery after marriage. It pushes avenues for seeking mental, if not physical pleasure outside of monogamous marriage. It popularizes seemingly innocuous practices like celebrity crushes. The world says that relational fulfillment can only be known in freedom from the shackles of monogamy. It is among the worst of lies.

The exact opposite is true. The most wildly fulfilling sexual relationship comes in the form that God prescribes—giving yourself totally and completely to one person till death do you part. Reserve your body, mind, and heart for your spouse, and you will be drunk with love.[8] This is God's design. The world's adulteration consisting of multiple partners and no commitment is the way of death.[9]

What if you've already violated God's good design? Chapter 13 will deal with this further, but, in short, *return to the gospel.* Jesus makes things new. Repent, seek forgiveness, get counseling, pursue Christ with a holy fervor, and recommit yourself to potent monogamy. There is nothing broken that Jesus cannot fix.

Third, we must enjoy a lifestyle of culmination. I used the absurd illustration earlier of someone entering marriage simply to escape singleness. No wedding night. No honeymoon. No intimacy with a spouse on any level. Most likely, no one intentionally begins a marriage that way, but there are many who end up there. For them, marriage has become simply the state of not being single. There was a time when they enjoyed intimacy with their spouse, but for whatever reasons, that intimacy atrophied. Now there is simply another person always around.

Such a state is unnatural. More significantly, it's ungodly and it defames the gospel. If marriage is intended to be a picture of the gospel, then a marriage wherein a husband and wife simply coexist lies about the nature of the relationship between Christ and the church. It is not the case that Jesus shed His blood and called a bride for Himself

---

[8] Pro. 5:18–19
[9] Pro. 5:1–15, 7:6–27

so that He and His bride could enjoy one another for a short season and then spend the rest of eternity in a condition of mutual indifference. No, sweet fellowship with Jesus is the entire point. It is what makes eternity desirable.

If our marriages would commend the gospel to an unbelieving world, our marriages cannot be ones in which intimacy takes place early on and then dies an unnatural and early death. Rather, they must be marriages in which intimacy is achieved and only grows sweeter and stronger with time.

A lifestyle of culmination should include growing spiritual, emotional, and sexual intimacy. These should be thought of as components of true intimacy rather than three separate activities. There is tremendous overlap and interplay among them. They both contribute to and are evidence of godly intimacy. Those who desire to enjoy the fullness of God's design should pursue depth in all three.

God created us as spiritual beings, and in Christ we have been brought from spiritual death to spiritual life. Therefore, to share with a person on the deepest level must entail spiritual connection. Spiritual intimacy entails enjoying Jesus together. Husbands and wives can do this by sharing Scripture with one another, praying together, and discussing the things of the Lord. Couples who worship Christ together will form the strongest of bonds.

We might think of emotional intimacy as the sharing of our hearts with one another—revealing our concerns, fears, and hopes to one another. Spiritual intimacy will only foster greater emotional intimacy. The closer we are to the Lord as a couple, the easier it will be to see our own hearts rightly and share them openly.

Sexual intimacy is far more than the physical pleasure derived from intercourse. It is the bodily expression of all the sharing taking place in a relationship. Where there is greater spiritual and emotional intimacy, the sexual act is likely to be more pleasurable and fulfilling. Where there is little or no spiritual or emotional intimacy, the sexual act will be nothing more than an orgasm. Ironically, the latter is the fool's gold that the world so desperately covets. Believers who have known the former wouldn't trade it for anything.

Over time, if we are committed to emulating the love of Christ, our marital intimacy should only grow stronger and more pleasurable.

This is time-consuming and requires intentionality. Left to themselves, our imperfectly sanctified hearts will regress to the extent that our marriages will be of the "I'm no longer single" variety. Intimacy will suffer and culmination will disappear. We must keep our eyes on Christ and purpose to love as He has loved us.

Likely, some reading this will think, "But you don't know how my spouse has hurt me." We're going to get to that in the next section of the Song. For now, consider this question: Are you so attached to your bitterness that you're willing to sacrifice the bliss of intimacy for it? Is your bitterness and unforgiveness so satisfying that you prefer it to joy? If the gospel is true, there is no such thing as a sin so big that it can prevent you from knowing fulfillment once again with your spouse. If Jesus Christ is the Lord of your life, you are obligated to pursue reconciliation and culmination with reckless abandon. The glorious wonder of it all is that He is so loving and generous that when you do, it will be delightful, both in your fellowship with Him and in your intimacy with your spouse.

If you don't go to that place of intimacy and savor it as a lifestyle with your spouse—sexually, spiritually, emotionally—you're not only failing to commend the gospel. Tragically, you're engaging in marriage as if still dead in your sins.

Choose to love your spouse. Choose potent monogamy. Choose a lifestyle of culmination. And thereby commend the gospel.

Discussion Questions/Activities

1. Knowing that His delight in you is based on His choice, not your perfection, does this change your intimacy with Him? How?

2. What in your life is threatening your monogamous worship of Christ? What specific steps can you take to remove these idols so that Christ alone is your hope?

3. At this point in the study, how is your fellowship with Christ growing? What practices have you implemented to enjoy Him? Do you conceive of Bible reading, prayer, and fellowship with the saints as avenues for enjoying the Lord, or tasks on a list? Be specific.

4. Are there forms of "soft" monogamy that you are tolerating in your marriage—ways in which you are perhaps physically faithful, but mentally or emotionally unfaithful? Confess this to your spouse. Talk to one another about what kind of help you might need (counseling, accountability relationships) to overcome these sinful habits.

5. Discuss the state of culmination in your marriage. Do you regularly enjoy spiritual intimacy? Emotional? Sexual? Is your marriage characterized by culmination or truncated crescendo? If truncated crescendo, how can you be more intentional about honoring the Lord in these areas?

10

FAILED & FOUND

Oxymoron

William Shakespeare loved oxymorons, or self-contradictory phrases, for their jarring, ironic effect. He strung thirteen together in one scene of Romeo & Juliet:

> O brawling love! O loving hate!
> O anything of nothing first create!
> O heavy lightness, serious vanity!
> Misshapen chaos of well-seeming forms!
> Feather of lead, bright smoke, cold fire, sick health!
> Still-waking sleep, that is not what it is!
> This love feel I, that feel no love in this.

Shakespeare isn't alone. Whether we do so intentionally or not, our written and oral communication is full of them.[1] Almost entirely. Only choice. Good grief. Virtual reality. Old news. Unbiased opinion. Larger half. Growing smaller. Soft rock. Minor miracle. Negative income. Live recording. Open secret. Random order. Working vacation. Exact estimate. Jumbo shrimp. Civil war. Crash landing.

---

[1] The word "oxymoron" is itself an oxymoron, derived from two Greek words meaning "sharp" and "dull."

Some of these we use intentionally to be ironic. We use others without even considering that they are self-contradictory. I'd like to add one to the latter category.

Irreconcilable marriage.

We have noted repeatedly that human marriage is intended to picture the gospel, the story of how the Father has reconciled sinners to himself by joining them to His Son. If it is the case that human marriage serves as a depiction of the gospel union of Christ and His bride, then marriage itself is about reconciliation. It exists as a testimony that though sin separates, the Savior restores; though rebellion marred God's good gifts, He makes all things new. Marriage is in this sense a celebration of and testimony to the blessedness of reconciliation.

Consider then the irony of ironies represented by any Christian marriage deemed to be irreconcilable. A marriage in which two people are at enmity is a living, breathing oxymoron. If we find ourselves unable to reconcile when we've wronged and been wronged, we've missed the point entirely. Understood within the appropriate gospel framework, an irreconcilable marriage is a contradiction in terms—an irreconcilable reconciliation.

Shakespeare may have loved the irony of a good oxymoron, but he was entertaining fallen people through tragedies that merely depict life's brokenness. God is writing a far better story, redeeming fallen people from tragic brokenness unto eternal reconciliation with Him. For His own glory and the good of His people, He has invested sinless blood and Holy Spirit power to ensure that no oxymoron mars marriage, this marquee picture of reconciliation.

Reconciliation—this may be the most critical component of learning to sing the Song of Songs. Just when we think we are at the brink of an irreconcilable marriage, the gospel shines its brightest, enabling the redeemed to do things the world finds unfathomable— repenting, denying self, forgiving, loving unconditionally, starting over with the same person, and doing so while clinging even more tightly to Christ than to a newly desirable spouse. If marriage depicts the gospel, marriage depicts reconciliation.

The Song (5:2–6:3)

(She)

2a I slept, but my heart was awake. A sound! My beloved is knocking.

(He)

2b "Open to me, my sister, my love, my dove, my perfect one, for my head is wet with dew, my locks with the drops of the night."

(She)

3 I had put off my garment; how could I put it on? I had bathed my feet; how could I soil them?

4 My beloved put his hand to the latch, and my heart was thrilled within me.

5 I arose to open to my beloved, and my hands dripped with myrrh, my fingers with liquid myrrh, on the handles of the bolt.

6 I opened to my beloved, but my beloved had turned and gone. My soul failed me when he spoke. I sought him, but found him not; I called him, but he gave no answer.

7 The watchmen found me as they went about in the city; they beat me, they bruised me, they took away my veil, those watchmen of the walls.

8 I adjure you, O daughters of Jerusalem, if you find my beloved, that you tell him I am sick with love.

(Chorus)

9 What is your beloved more than another beloved, O most beautiful among women? What is your beloved more than another beloved, that you thus adjure us?

(She)

10 My beloved is radiant and ruddy, distinguished among ten thousand.

11 His head is the finest gold; his locks are wavy, black as a raven.

12 His eyes are like doves beside streams of water, bathed in milk, sitting beside a full pool.

13 His cheeks are like beds of spices, mounds of sweet-smelling herbs. His lips are lilies, dripping liquid myrrh.

14 His arms are rods of gold, set with jewels. His body is polished ivory, bedecked with sapphires.

15 His legs are alabaster columns, set on bases of gold. His appearance is like Lebanon, choice as the cedars.

16 His mouth is most sweet, and he is altogether desirable. This is my beloved and this is my friend, O daughters of Jerusalem.

(Chorus)

6:1 Where has your beloved gone, O most beautiful among women? Where has your beloved turned, that we may seek him with you?

(She)

2 My beloved has gone down to his garden to the beds of spices, to graze in the gardens and to gather lilies.

3 I am my beloved's and my beloved is mine; he grazes among the lilies.

We're finally getting to what some might consider the most realistic scene in the whole Song. Thus far, we've encountered numerous idealized love scenes involving two spouses who adore each other. Now, just after the halfway point, just after the highest point of ecstasy in the Song, there is a bizarre failure. A point is being made, offering hope to those who have failed. Failure does not have to mean the end of bliss. Things can go back to the way they were. That is the message of the gospel and the message of this passage. Further, it can be the reality of your marriage. You may have failed your spouse and your spouse may have failed you, but what was lost can be found.

The woman begins, "I slept, but my heart was awake. A sound! My beloved is knocking. 'Open to me, my sister, my love, my dove, my perfect one, for my head is wet with dew, my locks with the drops of the night'" (5:2). The first sentence has led some to believe that this is a dream. However, it contains none of the typical Hebrew vocabulary of dreaming. Others think she is just sleeping lightly but is then awakened by his knocking. It's not crucial to make a hard case for either option; the message of the passage is the same. He knocks because he wants in. That's the important detail.

She continues in verse 3: "I had put off my garment; how could I put it on? I had bathed my feet; how could I soil them?" Many women can identify with this wife. Not only has she completed her before-bed routine, but she was already asleep. That her husband is covered in dew validates the view that he is coming at a late, inconvenient hour. She hesitates to get up and let him in because she doesn't want to get dressed or re-wash her feet. We are intended to recall the scene from chapter 3 where she was in bed, looking for him. There was no such thing as an inconvenience then. She simply took off in the middle of the night and went searching in the dark, dangerous streets.

This scene is a contrast. She knows where he is. He's right outside the door, and he wants in to be with her. Yet, initially she is slow to open the door for him.

With verse 4, she has an abrupt change of heart: "My beloved put his hand to the latch, and my heart was thrilled within me. I arose to open to my beloved, and my hands dripped with myrrh, my fingers with liquid myrrh, on the handles of the bolt." He's trying to open the door himself, and apparently this is enough to awaken her to her self-centeredness. Not only that, but she has such a change of heart that she begins to feel amorous. On her way to the door she dips her hands in myrrh, which chapter 1 revealed to be a perfume. Her hand is dripping with it as she reaches to open the door.

What will she find? "I opened to my beloved, but my beloved had turned and gone. My soul failed me when he spoke. I sought him, but found him not; I called him, but he gave no answer" (5:6). She waited too long. He gave up and went away. A crucial line in the whole scene is right in the middle of this verse—"My soul failed me when he spoke"—referring to when he was knocking on the door asking her to let him in. Rather than justifying her actions based upon the inconvenience of the hour, she takes responsibility for her actions. She realizes that he is gone because she failed to do the right thing. This man who so wonderfully loves her, who sees her as beautiful when she considers herself plain, whose love she has described as better than wine, and who considers her love to be equally delightful has potentially been lost because of her self-centeredness. *My soul failed me when he spoke.*

However, she does not collapse in despair, but in verse 7 goes out to seek him in the city, like chapter 3: "The watchmen found me as they went about in the city; they beat me, they bruised me, they took away my veil, those watchmen of the walls." Clearly, this is a departure from her midnight search earlier in the Song. We need to be careful not to treat this like a historical narrative. These are not real people. It's a song. We may want to ask questions like, "Why would the police beat this woman up in the middle of the city?" "Why would they beat her this time and not last time?" We don't have answers to those questions and looking for logical motivations and other such details will not lead us where we need to go. We must do a big-picture comparison between this scene and the similar scene in chapter 3. The big difference is that in chapter 3 she was self-sacrificing and did not suffer at the hands of the watchmen even though the opportunity was there; in chapter 5, she was self-centered and did suffer at the hands of the watchmen. At the very least, we can say that if she had let him in, she would not have needed to go looking for him, and there would have been no opportunity for her to be beaten by the watchmen. The beating is at least an indirect consequence of her failure.

This is such a dark scene in the middle of an idealized song. Yet, things do turn around, beginning in verse 8: "I adjure you, O daughters of Jerusalem, if you find my beloved, that you tell him I am sick with love." She enlists the help of the daughters of Jerusalem. The phrase "sick with love" is the same phrase she used back in chapter 2 in the passage about sitting under the shade of his apple tree. She's longing for better days. She wants to make things right.

The daughters respond in verse 9: "What is your beloved more than another beloved, O most beautiful among women? What is your beloved more than another beloved, that you thus adjure us?" Her previous admonitions to them have been exclusively, "Save yourself for marriage, save yourself for marriage."[2] Now she says, "If you see my beloved, tell him that I'm sick with love." The former seems to be

---

[2] Of course, this is my interpretation of those previous addresses in 2:7 and 3:5. The actual text in both places reads, "I adjure you, O daughters of Jerusalem, by the gazelles or the does of the field, that you not stir up or awaken love until it pleases."

a very serious admonition; the second somewhat frivolous. Therefore, they're wondering, "What's so wonderful about this guy that you would make us swear to do this?"

Note also that this is the first time they call her "Most beautiful among women." Prior to this, only her husband referred to her this way. How interesting that they call her this at this point in the Song. She's just been beaten and bruised by the watchmen, and yet, they're calling her, "O most beautiful among women." What might we gather from this? She is doing a beautiful thing by pursuing her husband, returning to the tenacity she had back in chapter 3. In the process, she has been beaten by strangers. Many, many people would give up the search at that point, but she doesn't. In fact, we might say that she has become even more tenacious than she was in chapter 3 in that here she enlists help in finding him. This is a beautiful thing—she has failed but will not give up.

In the following verses, she answers their question:

> My beloved is radiant and ruddy, distinguished among ten thousand. His head is the finest gold; his locks are wavy, black as a raven. His eyes are like doves beside streams of water, bathed in milk, sitting beside a full pool. His cheeks are like beds of spices, mounds of sweet-smelling herbs. His lips are lilies, dripping liquid myrrh. His arms are rods of gold, set with jewels. His body is polished ivory, bedecked with sapphires. His legs are alabaster columns, set on bases of gold. His appearance is like Lebanon, choice as the cedars. His mouth is most sweet, and he is altogether desirable. This is my beloved and this is my friend, O daughters of Jerusalem (5:10-16).

The point is captured by the summary in verse 16: "He is altogether desirable." She's rehearsing what she stands to lose if she does not find him and make things right. He is her "beloved" and her "friend." Those two words encompass the totality of their union. Remember, their question was, "What is your beloved more than another beloved, that you thus adjure us?" (5:9). With the last sentence of verse 16, her answer is, "He's altogether desirable. He's my friend. He's mine. I don't want to lose him."

The daughters of Jerusalem understand and offer to help in 6:1: "Where has your beloved gone, O most beautiful among women? Where has your beloved turned, that we may seek him with you?" She responds: "My beloved has gone down to his garden to the beds of spices, to graze in the gardens and to gather lilies. I am my beloved's and my beloved is mine; he grazes among the lilies" (6:2). This seems like an abrupt resolution of the situation. A great search is under way, the woman asks the daughters of Jerusalem to help her, and they agree, asking, "Where has he gone that we may seek him with you?" Suddenly, in 6:2, he's already been found. It may be more accurate to say he found her.

Again, this is not an historical narrative, so it shouldn't trouble us for there not to be a tight, logical sequence of events. Clearly, even though it is not depicted, they have found one another again, and they have reconciled. The language of 6:2 indicates that they are doing their favorite thing again, with verse 3 showing that things have been completely restored. Verse 3 is an almost verbatim repetition of 2:16. "I am my beloved's and my beloved is mine; he grazes among the lilies." Everything has been restored to the way it was before. What they had before the failure has been found again.

Consider three truths gathered from this scene. **First, marital love, as God intended, owns personal failure.** She recognizes what she's done and moves to rectify it. "My soul failed me when he spoke" (5:6). Then she takes off to find him.

Second, marital love, as God intended, recognizes the value of what can be lost to sin. So many lines are dedicated to answering the question of the chorus in this passage. "What's so wonderful about this man that you thus adjure us?" She recognizes what she stands to lose, and it motivates her to make things right even after she's been brutalized by the watchmen of the city.

Third, marital love, as God intended, reconciles. This episode of failure does not permanently impede their intimacy. Failure didn't create a new normal. Their original joy and intimacy were found again.

Christ, Waiting at the Door

Obviously, the beginning of our relationship with the Lord Jesus represented a reconciliation between us and the Father. We were conceived estranged from God. Yet by His providential plan and through the life, atoning death, and resurrection of Christ, our sins have been forgiven and we have been reconciled to God through repentance and faith.

However, all of us know that even after our conversion, we continue to have hearts prone to wander. We tend toward indifference toward Jesus. As with this woman in chapter 5, the joy of fellowship with the Bridegroom so easily cools to complacency. We become comfortable in our reconciliation, so comfortable that we cease to be amazed by it.

Like the man in the Song, Christ knocks at the door. Most believers will have heard Revelation 3:20 before: "Behold, I stand at the door and knock. If anyone hears my voice and opens the door, I will come in to him and eat with him, and he with me." Typically, this verse is used as a tool for evangelism. However, those are the words of the Lord Jesus to lukewarm believers in the church at Laodicea. There, Jesus is not calling unbelievers to be saved, but the saved to return to Him. They had become indifferent toward Him, but He portrays Himself as outside the door, desiring fellowship with them. All they must do to enjoy Him is to open the door. Given the numerous depictions of the church as the bride of Christ in Revelation, I believe the Lord intentionally draws on the Song there in Revelation 3:20.[3]

As in the Song, Jesus does not always come on our preferred terms and at our preferred time. Frequently, discipleship will be inconvenient to say the least. In a world clamoring for our attention and affections, it takes effort to devote ourselves to fellowship with the Lord Jesus. However, even in the most inconvenient moments and seasons, we should open the door to Him. When we do, we will find joy. When we don't, we will know regret.

Like the woman, we make Him wait. We have other concerns—social media to peruse, Netflix to binge, careers to build, dreams to entertain, bitterness to nurse—a million mildly interesting things that call our attention to ourselves and away from the Lord of Glory who bought us. Whether these distractions are inherently sinful

---

[3] Rev. 19:7, 9; 21:2, 9; 22:17

or not, they remove from us any sense of urgency to open the door. Our passion for the Lord wanes and our false worship grows, which can lead to catastrophic results.

David knew the terrible consequences of such distractions. After running for his life for many years, David enjoyed rest from all his enemies and eventually became quite comfortable in his stature as king.[4] It was in the context of this leisure that he let down his guard spiritually and fell into the sin that almost came to define him. 2 Samuel 11 describes David's adulterous relationship with Bathsheba and his murdering her husband, Uriah. In Psalm 51, we read about David's heart when he realized the depth of his sin. We might have expected David, like Adam, to shift the blame— "Lord, she was bathing in broad daylight. Cut me some slack."[5] Blessedly, David owned the blame for his sin: "I know my transgressions, and my sin is ever before me. Against you, you only, have I sinned and done what is evil in your sight" (Psa. 51:3–4a).

David also fully appreciated what he stood to lose— "Restore to me the joy of your salvation…" (Psa. 51:12). When we shut Jesus out, worshiping other gods in His place, entertaining unrepentant sin and allowing other things to become more desirable to us than He is, there can be a host of consequences. It can lead to depression or the loss of the joy of our salvation. It can lead to the searing of our conscience, inhibition in our worship, and lack of assurance. Perhaps worst of all, we can arrive at a long-term coldness that convinces us that this is all that the Christian life can ever be. Like David, like the woman of the Song, we must own our failures and appreciate what we stand to lose—the fullness of fellowship that Christ gave Himself to provide.

The key to repaired fellowship is not simply to do better or to sin less, but to recognize we have failed to see the value of Jesus Himself. The woman in the Song does not say, "Oh, that was wrong. I should have let him in. Boy, I'm gonna try harder to let him in next time." No, she is re-awakened to the beauty of her husband and the joy of knowing him. She's horrified that she may have jeopardized her

---

[4] 2 Sam. 7:9–11; 8:1–14; 10:1–11:1

[5] Our first father Adam was the original blame-shifter, seeking to unload culpability both on God and Eve - "The woman whom *you* gave to be with me, *she* gave me the fruit of the tree, and I ate" (Gen. 3:12).

intimacy with him. "This is my beloved, and this is my friend..." (5:16).

We would do well to think in the same terms. The reason sin is so horrible, as a believer, is that it impedes our ability to enjoy Jesus. Not only that, we would do well to list and meditate on His attributes. As the wife has seemingly no trouble listing a host of reasons to find her husband worth pursuing, how much more do we have reason to desire greater knowledge of the Lord Jesus? We can mentally recite His excellencies—humility, compassion, wisdom, generosity, power, forgiveness, faithfulness, longsuffering, authority, submission, and kindness—by returning to the gospel over and over, reading the Old Testament with a Christological focus (as we are doing with the Song), and slowly reading the Gospel narratives while letting the epistles fill them with theological insight.

The gospel—no matter where in the Scriptures we find it—keeps us mindful of how eager He is to forgive. It keeps us mindful of how there is no such thing as a sin too big for Him to cover with His blood and restore us to fellowship. We have committed countless adulteries against our Savior, and yet He repeatedly, eagerly receives us back. We fail Him, but He finds us.

Prescription for Healing

Every couple has experienced the sting of a spouse's sin *and* has committed those stinging sins. It's a great tragedy that believers, of all people, can eventually arrive at a place where they believe their marriage is irreconcilable. That kind of thinking— "My marriage has failed; it can't be fixed"—misses the connection between human marriage and the gospel. Christ is powerful to save and sanctify those who formerly hated God and one another. A blessed implication of this truth is that husbands and wives can be changed and reconciled to one another. There is no marriage that is beyond Christ's power to repair. We have only to follow His prescription.

That prescription could be administered in three parts. **First, we must own our personal failures.** Marital love, as God intended, owns personal failure. That's just another way of saying, it confesses and repents. That seems like a simple concept, but one of the most common themes in marital strife is what I would call, "Yeah, but you…" "I did this, but you did that… I only did what I did because of what you did to me…" In the mouth of the woman of the Song, this might sound like, "I would have opened the door to you if you'd come home earlier…"

Essentially, the great temptation is to get our spouses to take ownership for our failures. "You caused me to do what I did." If you can't hear echoes of the fallen Adam in that statement, let me turn up the volume a bit: "The woman whom you gave to be with me, she gave me fruit of the tree, and I ate" (Gen. 3:12). The Lord sees through these attempts to justify ourselves by the sins of others. No one can make me sin; I do it because I want to. I alone am responsible for my sin.

"But Greg, my spouse's sin is not just a simple matter of having failed to unlock the door for me, as in the Song. My spouse cheated on me. My spouse lied to me." There could be any number of other very serious sins represented here. It's not my aim to minimize any of them, nor is it my desire to minimize the pain that sin has caused you. I also don't want to imply that overcoming that pain and those sinful patterns is as simple as confession, repentance, and forgiveness. There are some issues in marriages that require the outside help of pastors and counseling. It may take some time.

Regardless of the situation, gospel-centered people do not settle for a marriage in which unreconciled hurts are the norm; they pursue godly intimacy as depicted in the Song. The Lord Jesus saved us so that we would no longer live for ourselves, but for Him who for our sake died and was raised.[6] Living in bitterness and unrepentance simply is not an option for those who truly belong to Christ. If we would be faithful, we must pursue reconciliation.

Your spouse may have committed adultery and lied, among other horrible things. Your spouse needs to take ownership of those sins. But in what ways have *you* sinned? Your spouse did not cause you to sin; you sinned because you desired it. Therefore, you must repent and seek forgiveness. Bear in mind that your sin is not simply a sin against your spouse, but more importantly, against God. You can't be right with God while there is unforgiveness between you and your spouse.

---

[6] 2 Cor. 5:15

If any marriage is going to be a godly one, each spouse must take responsibility for his/her own sins. Each must repent without reference to the sins of the other. "I sinned by doing this to you. I did it of my own choice. I was wrong. I repent. I don't want to do it again. Will you please forgive me?" Repentance is a beautiful thing when you realize that it leads to reconciliation between you and the Lord as well as between you and your spouse.

A second part of God's prescription is recognizing the value of what might be lost to our sin. The woman in the Song, as she recounts the description of her husband, says he is too wonderful to lose. We need to recognize what we stand to lose by tolerating a climate of estrangement in our marriages.

Of course, some of us might say, "What I have is not too wonderful to lose. In fact, I'd feel quite free if I lost it." In your private moments, you may even have daydreamed about that—being free of your spouse. Out of love, I want to point out two ways in which your thinking can become more gospel-minded.

Number one: Focus on what you could have, instead of what you currently have. The gospel changes people. Growth in Christlikeness is the norm, by God's grace. Paul taught that God is determined—and has been from eternity past—to conform believers into the image of Christ.[7] Since that is true, it is illogical to believe that your marriage now is what your marriage will be in the future.

The fact that we give up so easily, that we believe things could never get better, demonstrates that despite what we say on Sunday morning and sing in our songs, we really believe in a tiny Jesus who can't save anyone and who makes nothing new. Wouldn't it be absurd to believe Him capable of rescuing us from eternal, omnipotent wrath, but not from a lousy character? The Christ who saves also sanctifies! This is fantastic news for the future of every Christian marriage.

Right now, in your mind, you may think that the greatest source of your suffering is your spouse. What if your biggest problem is a chronic underestimation of the gospel? What if the biggest failure of your marriage is your mutual failing to really believe that Jesus is

---

[7] Rom. 8:29

mighty to save, He makes all things new, and His strength is sufficient in our weakness?

This is not to suggest that you adopt a name-it-and-claim-it position regarding your marriage. Rather, adopt a truly outrageous and counter-cultural posture—believe the gospel is true! Believe that the Holy Spirit can change hearts, even yours. Believe that He can change your spouse's heart, and that even if He doesn't, He will give you the grace and strength necessary to love as you've been called to love. This is not a fairy tale; we've discarded those. This is believing in the gospel promises of God.[8] Don't focus on what you currently have, but on what you could have because the gospel is true.

Number two: Consider what commends the gospel. If you're a disciple of Jesus Christ, your entire existence is about making Him known. Whether or not your marriage ever improves as a result of your obedience should be secondary in your mind. Primary ought to be, "What can I do in my marriage to demonstrate the truthfulness of the gospel?"

Jesus said, "If anyone would come after me, let him deny himself and take up his cross and follow me" (Matt. 16:24). You don't belong to you; you've been bought with a price.[9] Your marriage doesn't belong to you; it's God's display of His kindness in Christ.[10] Therefore, you do not have the right to settle for a marriage where unreconciled hurts are allowed to lay around like a decomposing body. Why? Because that kind of marriage lies to the world about the gospel.

What does that kind of marriage say to the world about the gospel? First, it says that Jesus is okay with estrangement. Nothing could be further from the truth. He poured out His blood so that our reconciliation could be absolute, and so that we could be reconciled to one another. Second, it paints a picture of a Jesus whose fellowship we can do without. If you can do without your spouse's fellowship, you're acting out a gospel of the same caliber, saying, "Jesus is not so desirable that I'm really missing anything when I don't have Him." We would never say something so blasphemous, yet our marriages may be depicting that very thing.

---

[8] Eze. 11:19–20, 36:26–27; 2 Cor. 12:9–10; 1 John 4:19
[9] 1 Cor. 6:19–20
[10] Eph. 5:32

So, consider the value of what could be lost to your unreconciled sin. You're turning away from the potential of marital bliss as depicted in the Song, and you're losing the glorious privilege of accurately depicting the gospel. Decide that these are intolerable eventualities.

The third part of God's prescription is striving for the joy of reconciliation. Have you ever thought about how often pain and struggle precede the greatest joys of life? Those who arrive at joy do so not by focusing on the struggle, but on the destination. The woman with a severe brain injury will never learn to walk again if all she can see is the long, arduous hours of physical therapy, waiting for her brain to make the necessary connections. She will only get there if she imagines the bliss of putting one foot in front of the other unassisted.

The Bible puts this principle in front of us numerous times. Jesus warned His disciples about the sorrow they would experience when He was crucified. Using the metaphor of childbirth, He called on them to endure those dark days by looking forward to the joy of His resurrection: "When a woman is giving birth, she has sorrow because her hour has come, but when she has delivered the baby, she no longer remembers the anguish, for joy that a human being has been born into the world" (John 16:21).

We have no better example of the principle than Jesus Himself, "…the founder and perfecter of our faith, who for the joy that was set before him endured the cross, despising the shame, and is seated at the right hand of the throne of God" (Heb. 12:2). There was nothing pleasurable about the final hours of Jesus' life. All His friends abandoned Him. He was charged with, convicted of, and sentenced to death for crimes He never committed. He endured sleep deprivation, dehydration, and physical pain so terrible that His manner of death (crucifixion) spawned a term—excruciating—which we now use to describe the height of suffering. Worst of all, the sinless One experienced an agony you and I cannot imagine, as His infinitely sensitive conscience bore the guilt of every vile act of the world, and with it, the Father's wrath.

How did He complete this mission? After all, He could have put an end to the whole thing.[11] How did He "endure the cross, despising

---

[11] He told Pilate He had the authority to call more than 12 legions of angels to assist Him. (Matt. 26:53)

the shame"? According to the author of Hebrews, it was for the joy set before Him.

What joy? The joy of reconciliation! We are not left to wonder what Jesus desired on the other side of the cross:

> I do not ask for these [disciples] only, but also for those who will believe in me through their word, that they may all be one, just as you, Father, are in me, and I in you, that they also may be in us... Father, I desire that they also, whom you have given me, may be with me where I am, to see my glory that you have given me because you loved me before the foundation of the world (John 17:20–21, 24).

Jesus wanted to spend eternity with us. There was one enormous problem; we were sinners estranged from the Father. Reconciliation was not only necessary, but would be painful, as well. However, to Jesus the joy was so worthwhile that nothing could keep Him from the cross. In fact, He was determined to go there. "I lay down my life that I may take it up again. No one takes it from me, but I lay it down of my own accord" (John 10:17–18).

Consider this, brothers and sisters: if our Lord considered the joy of spending eternity with us worth enduring the wrath of the Almighty, ought we not consider the joy of a marriage like the Song worth the relatively light pain of repenting of our own sin and forgiving those committed against us? Accordingly, for the joy set before us, like Christ, we should strive for reconciliation, enduring whatever is necessary.

Often the largest and most difficult part of striving for reconciliation is forgiving one another. When we forgive, we are saying, "I no longer hold this sin against you." Practically, this means not using the sin as weapon in future arguments, not discussing the sin with others, and—the really hard one—not dwelling on the sin in our own minds.[12] However, there is no such thing as reconciliation without forgiveness. I dare say it is not possible for a true believer to

---

[12] Sadly, there is great confusion in the modern church about what biblical forgiveness is. Therefore, I highly recommend this book: Chris Brauns, *Unpacking Forgiveness: Biblical Answers For Complex Questions And Deep Wounds* (Wheaton, IL: Crossway, 2008).

say, "I cannot forgive you."[13] Jesus would never minimize the pain your spouse's sin has caused you. He knows better than you do the offense of that sin—He died for it. He is perfectly situated to help you forgive, and He calls you to do so.

Oh, the heart of Christ toward those who sin against Him and repent! All of Luke 15 contains the Lord's parables to the effect that "there will be more joy in heaven over one sinner who repents than over ninety-nine righteous persons who need no repentance" (Luke 15:7). Let those who would strive for reconciliation in their broken marriages consciously strive for the heart of Christ. He loved so intensely that the joy over having found what was lost eclipsed the offense of any sin committed by the repentant. Pray, pray, pray for that kind of love. He is the kind of Savior who will give it.

It is not the seriousness of the sin that determines whether a marriage is destroyed or thrives. Some marriages have been destroyed by nothing more than poor communication, while others have thrived after being rocked by adultery. It's not the seriousness of the sin—it's the willingness of the husband and wife to strive for the joy set before them. Those marriages in which both spouses recognize their own failures, recognize the value of what could be lost, and strive for the joy of reconciliation are the marriages that are able to overcome sin and thrive. That is the power of gospel-infused reconciliation. It is available to everyone who believes. Because Christ is our beloved and our friend, there is no marriage beyond saving.

Discussion Questions/Activities

1. Do you see that Christ's knocking on the door of your life is always a wonderful opportunity? Do you sometimes expect Him to come on your terms? What if He knocks when it is inconvenient?

2. Would you say you are currently keeping Him waiting, or enjoying fellowship with Him? If the former, what would this scene call you to do specifically?

---

[13] Matt. 6:15; 18:23–35.

3. Do you believe that Jesus is always eager to forgive and be reconciled? How does this motivate you?

4. In what ways is it a denial of the gospel to withhold forgiveness from a spouse who has hurt you? Does the magnitude or number of hurts change this? Why or why not?

5. It's a great practice to regularly just sit down together and ask, "Do we have any unreconciled issues? Is there anything we need to talk about?" Do that now with your spouse.

6. Are there any past hurts that continue to plague your marriage? Should you consider getting counseling?

11

TRANSFIXED & TRANSFORMED

The Mirror Has Two Faces

Over the years, I've been a member of several gyms and they all have one thing in common. They cover the walls in mirrors. Every indication is that people appreciate this. Folks seem to be mesmerized by watching themselves change, which is an apparent motivation to keep working hard. "I look better than I did a month ago. Imagine how good I'll look a month from now!" There is no other public place where it is so acceptable—even expected—to gaze at yourself in awe.

For people like me, the mirrors only serve as a constant reminder of how cavalierly I squandered the testosterone of my youth. I only started exercising on the back side of that very steep hill. For that reason, I do my best not to gaze at myself while exercising—there's no motivation there.

However, I inadvertently saw something in the mirror at the gym a few days ago. I caught a glimpse of myself walking to the locker room, and I thought, "My soul, I walk just like Moe!" Moe is my youngest son and the baby of the family. It was a surreal moment. People have told me many times that we look alike and have the same mannerisms, but I'd never seen it for myself. I realized, of course, that Moe really walks like me, but initially it was the mirror that made me think the opposite—that I walk like him. I was looking in a mirror, but seeing my son, in a sense.

I immediately texted my wife:

Just saw myself in a mirror walking. I walk just like Moe.
I wanted to hug myself.

She understood what I meant. Seeing that gait made me want to throw my arms around him, not only because I was reminded of him, but because I felt closer to him as a result of seeing how obviously connected we are. It's a strange thing to look in a mirror, see yourself, and feel affection for *someone else*.

Transfixed & Transformed in the Song

This is exactly where the woman of the Song will eventually find herself—recognizing her own image, she will see her resemblance to the beauty of her husband. Rather than being taken with herself, she will become more enamored with him.

To this point, the woman obviously has been transfixed by her husband's love. In chapter 1, she extolled his desirability, his inherent beauty, saying that she was not alone in seeing it, that all the girls adored him. The daughters of Jerusalem backed her up in 1:4, "We will exult and rejoice in you; we will extol your love more than wine; rightly do they love you." He is universally attractive and desirable.

Remember that she is not. "Do not gaze at me because I am dark, because the sun has looked upon me" (1:6). Therefore, at the outset of the Song it appears that these two are somewhat oddly matched. He is inherently desirable; she is unattractive. He is exactly what a woman would want. She is exactly what no man would want.

Yet, from the very first time the husband opened his mouth in the Song, it has been clear that she is beautiful to him. With his very first line he calls her "O most beautiful among women" (1:8). It's no wonder that she is transfixed by his love and that she loves him in return. Early in the Song, her great affection for him was highlighted in that she did the lion's share of speaking. In chapter 3, when she looked for him in the night and didn't find him, she took off into the dangerous darkness to find him. She's obsessed with him. He is the object of her highest affections. She's transfixed.

Yet, with each time he extols her beauty, we remember the reality of her station. She's actually unattractive. We're left to assume that her

husband has been blinded by love and that this blind love has led to
her being transfixed by him.

However, in chapter 5, it appears there may be a transformation
taking place in her. The woman failed her husband, but in her pursuit
of him, the chorus twice called her "O most beautiful among women"
(5:9, 6:1). Is it possible that she is not only beautiful in her husband's
eyes because of his love, but that she has been transformed so that
others also see her as beautiful? The present text indicates that she has.
She has become like the object of her highest affections. As she has
been transfixed, she has been transformed.

The Song (6:4–8:4)
(He)

*6:4 You are beautiful as Tirzah, my love, lovely as Jerusalem,
awesome as an army with banners.*

*5 Turn away your eyes from me, for they overwhelm me—Your
hair is like a flock of goats leaping down the slopes of Gilead.*

*6 Your teeth are like a flock of ewes that have come up from the
washing; all of them bear twins; not one among them has lost its
young.*

7 Your cheeks are like halves of a pomegranate behind your veil.

*8 There are sixty queens and eighty concubines, and virgins without
number.*

*9 My dove, my perfect one, is the only one, the only one of her
mother, pure to her who bore her. The young women saw her and
called her blessed; the queens and concubines also, and they
praised her.*

*10 "Who is this who looks down like the dawn, beautiful as the
moon, bright as the sun, awesome as an army with banners?"*

(She)

*11 I went down to the nut orchard to look at the blossoms of the
valley, to see whether the vines had budded, whether the
pomegranates were in bloom.*

*12 Before I was aware, my desire set me among the chariots of my
kinsman, a prince.*

(Chorus)

13 Return, return, O Shulammite, return, return, that we may look upon you.

(He)

    Why should you look upon the Shulammite, as upon a dance before two armies?

7:1 How beautiful are your feet in sandals, O noble daughter! Your rounded thighs are like jewels, the work of a master hand.

2 Your navel is a rounded bowl that never lacks mixed wine. Your belly is a heap of wheat, encircled with lilies.

3 Your two breasts are like two fawns, twins of a gazelle.

4 Your neck is like an ivory tower. Your eyes are pools in Heshbon, by the gate of Bath-rabbim. Your nose is like a tower of Lebanon, which looks toward Damascus.

5 Your head crowns you like Carmel, and your flowing locks are like purple; a king is held captive in the tresses.

6 How beautiful and pleasant you are, O loved one, with all your delights!

7 Your stature is like a palm tree, and your breasts are like its clusters.

8 I say I will climb the palm tree and lay hold of its fruit. Oh may your breasts be like clusters of the vine, and the scent of your breath like apples,

9a and your mouth like the best wine.

(She)

9b It goes down smoothly for my beloved, gliding over lips and teeth.

10 I am my beloved's, and his desire is for me.

11 Come, my beloved, let us go out into the fields and lodge in the villages;

12 let us go out early to the vineyards and see whether the vines have budded, whether the grape blossoms have opened and the pomegranates are in bloom. There I will give you my love.

13 The mandrakes give forth fragrance, and beside our doors are all choice fruits, new as well as old, which I have laid up for you, O my beloved.

8:1 Oh that you were like a brother to me who nursed at my mother's breasts! If I found you outside, I would kiss you, and none would despise me.

2 I would lead you and bring you into the house of my mother— she who used to teach me. I would give you spiced wine to drink, the juice of my pomegranate.

3 His left hand is under my head, and his right hand embraces me!

4 I adjure you, O daughters of Jerusalem, that you not stir up or awaken love until it pleases.

This is by far the longest text that we will cover in one piece— two full chapters of the Song. Because much of what is written in these chapters is a verbatim repetition of what has come before, we will not go over each verse closely. The point of the chapters is found by comparing them to the larger context. Once again, the point made centers on the effect that the husband's love has on the wife: she is transfixed and transformed.

A Gracious Transformation

The passage begins with 6:4–7, a near verbatim repetition from chapter 4. Why would the husband do this? Doesn't he know that rote expressions of praise lose their luster? Well, this takes place right after her failure in chapter 5. If he's complimenting her in the same way that he did before that failure, it means that there has been complete restoration. She is as beautiful to him now as she was before she left him in the cold. He has completely forgiven her.

Verses 8–14 are where her transformation shines. First, verses 8–10:

There are sixty queens and eighty concubines, and virgins without number. My dove, my perfect one, is the only one, the only one of her mother, pure to her who bore her. The young women saw her and called her blessed; the queens and concubines also, and they praised her. "Who is this who looks down like the dawn, beautiful as the moon, bright as the sun, awesome as an army with banners?"

Once again, the author Solomon inserts himself into the story as a foil for the love of the man and woman. The reference to the queens and concubines is a reference to his extravagant, yet impersonal, non-monogamous love life. The husband of the Song points to that harem and says to his wife, "Solomon has women without number, but you are singular to me." Additionally, the husband points out that she is superior to all of Solomon's women in that they all look at her, call her blessed, and praise her. Consider what a drastic change in circumstances this is. Earlier she said, "Don't look at me; I'm damaged by the sun." Now, other women gaze at her and adore her.

To call her "blessed" is to say she has been *given* blessings. She has been blessed by being loved so well by this man. She has been acted upon by something outside of herself, and yet they praise *her*—specifically, her inherent beauty in verse 10. That is striking. She is no longer treated as culturally unattractive. Rather, she is praised as he was at the beginning of the Song. It is clear then that she is beautiful because something has acted upon her. His great love for her has transformed her so that she is now truly beautiful...and *she* is praised for it.

In verses 11–12, she describes how her transformation came about. She was looking for love and found herself among a noble people.[1] We should note that he uses the same word—noble—to describe her in 7:1. These are the only two times the word is used in the whole Song. She went looking for love and found herself among this noble people, being loved by this noble man, thus, she became noble. Implied is that he is the transforming agent.

With verse 13, the chorus chimes in: "Return, return, O Shulammite, return, return, that we may look upon you." She's so beautiful that they call her back that they may admire her beauty still.

---

[1] The ESV is the only major translation to translate v12 as, "among the chariots of my kinsman, a prince." Most others render it something like "among the chariots of my noble people." For that reason, here I have used "people."

This emphasizes again that she has become like him. They are praising her the way they praised him at the beginning of the Song.[2]

Taken together, verses 8–13 emphasize her transformation. She has actually become beautiful, and given the entire context, this transformation seems to be the result of his love resting on her. Even his lengthy lauding of her beauty beginning in chapter 7 serves to highlight this transformation. Consider 7:1–9a altogether:

> How beautiful are your feet in sandals, O noble daughter! Your rounded thighs are like jewels, the work of a master hand. Your navel is a rounded bowl that never lacks mixed wine. Your belly is a heap of wheat, encircled with lilies. Your two breasts are like two fawns, twins of a gazelle. Your neck is like an ivory tower. Your eyes are pools in Heshbon, by the gate of Bathrabbim. Your nose is like a tower of Lebanon, which looks toward Damascus. Your head crowns you like Carmel, and your flowing locks are like purple; a king is held captive in the tresses. How beautiful and pleasant you are, O loved one, with all your delights! Your stature is like a palm tree, and your breasts are like its clusters. I say I will climb the palm tree and lay hold of its fruit. Oh may your breasts be like clusters of the vine, and the scent of your breath like apples, and your mouth like the best wine.

Let's recognize once again that we can't take these metaphors and transplant them into modern-day America. Try these with your wife and see where it gets you—particularly, "your belly is a heap of wheat." (Free advice: don't ever use the word "heap" with your wife.)

After getting over how obtuse these compliments sound, we may be overwhelmed by the task of understanding each one of them. However, that is not where the main points are found in this text. Here is the true gem of these metaphors: the whole section is strikingly similar to and yet slightly different from the crescendo and culmination passage in chapter 4. It is the difference that is significant.

---

[2] He rebukes the chorus in v13b. Almost no commentator knows what to make of the last phrase in v13—"as a dance before two armies." A loose consensus regarding the meaning of the rebuke is that she does not exist for their viewing pleasure.

In both passages, he demonstrates he is enthralled with her beauty, using many repeated phrases. In both passages, he expresses in somewhat explicit terms his desire to enjoy her sexually. In both passages, her essential reply is, "I'm all yours; enjoy yourself."

The significance is in the *difference* in the two passages created by a different opening and a different conclusion. First, just before this escalation we see the chorus praising her inherent beauty. That is, we see that she has been transformed. Second, as the woman replies in 7:10, we find a modified version of the Song's refrain, "I am my beloved's, *and his desire is for me.*" But what is the typical refrain? "I am my beloved's and my beloved is mine." With the modified refrain—"*and his desire is for me*"—her beauty, her inherent desirability is emphasized. "*He truly desires me. He's pleased with me.*"

Prior to this, he expressed desire for her, but she was described in the text as inherently unattractive. That has changed now. Now, she believes that he truly does desire her rather than being blinded by love, in a sense. The repetition of his words shows that he does not love her more now that she has been transformed. He loves her just like he always did. And, certainly, he is pleased by her beauty, but that's nothing new. Still, she has been transformed. She is truly beautiful.

What would you expect of a woman who has suddenly realized that she is truly beautiful and everyone thinks so? You might expect her to become consumed with herself. Not the woman of the Song. She becomes all the more transfixed by her husband. Perhaps this is for two reasons. First, he is the agent of her transformation. Second, her transformation is not what moved him to love her. For these reasons, she is overwhelmed by passion for this man as evidenced in verses 9b through 8:4.

All the More Transfixed

It goes down smoothly for my beloved, gliding over lips and teeth. I am my beloved's, and his desire is for me. Come, my beloved, let us go out into the fields and lodge in the villages; let us go out early to the vineyards and see whether the vines have budded, whether the grape blossoms have opened and the pomegranates are in bloom. There I will give you my love. The mandrakes give forth fragrance, and beside our doors are all

choice fruits, new as well as old, which I have laid up for you, O my beloved.
Oh that you were like a brother to me who nursed at my mother's breasts! If I found you outside, I would kiss you, and none would despise me. I would lead you and bring you into the house of my mother—she who used to teach me. I would give you spiced wine to drink, the juice of my pomegranate. His left hand is under my head, and his right hand embraces me! I adjure you, O daughters of Jerusalem, that you not stir up or awaken love until it pleases (7:9b–8:4).

These verses show the woman expressing her desire to enjoy her husband all the more, which presents a contrast to the progression of chapter 4. In chapter 4, after the original crescendo and culmination, she became indifferent toward her husband. Now, in the wake of her transformation, there is a repeated crescendo and culmination, not followed by indifference, but rather by an intensified desire for her husband. She has not become consumed with herself, but with him. She's all the more transfixed. The metaphors in those verses are not veiled. She's saying, "Let's do our thing, shall we?"

Now, 8:1 is puzzling to many people. It sounds as if she is saying, "Oh, I wish you were my brother," which doesn't sound terribly romantic. However, in the ancient Near East it was not culturally appropriate to be overtly affectionate in public with one's spouse, while it was acceptable to show affection with a family member. She's simply saying, "I'm so nuts about you, I don't want to only be affectionate with you in private. I want the freedom to be affectionate with you in public. I want to be able to kiss you in front of people. I would kiss you publicly and then [v2] I would take you to mom's house and we would do things privately."

The words of 8:3, we've seen before in chapter 2. It's a repetition of the lover's embrace described there, which is why once again, she calls the daughters of Jerusalem to save themselves for marriage in verse 4. His love has transformed her; he is pleased by it, and yet the transformation is not the reason for his love. This moves her to be all the more transfixed by him.

The Transforming Object of Our Affections

Now that we have read so much of the Song Christologically, it may be quite natural to see how Jesus exemplifies the love in this section. Quite simply, He transforms us. This is a beautiful, but perhaps often overlooked aspect of the gospel.

From our conception, we were estranged from God. Our rebellion against His holy character rightfully resulted in our being under His holy wrath. Yet God moved to save us by sending His Son to live righteously in our place and to die on the cross, enduring the penalty for our sin. Three days later, the Father raised Jesus from the dead, demonstrating that Jesus was indeed the Son of God and that His sacrifice was sufficient to pay for the sins of His people. Everyone who repents of sin and trusts in Jesus is united to Christ, forgiven of sin, and enjoys all of Christ's eternal blessings with Him forever. Our salvation is a function of our sin becoming His and His righteousness becoming ours. We wear His righteousness. We call this the imputed righteousness of Christ.

Until now, we have related the beauty of the woman in the Song to this imputed righteousness of Christ. She is beautiful because her husband has covered her with his love. This is a glorious truth. However, there is something more that Jesus does for us. He does not only clothe us with His righteousness, but He also *transforms* us into His image. He makes us like Him. Romans 8:28–30 teaches that one of the great eternal purposes of God is to conform believers to the image of Christ.

Second Corinthians 3:18 shows the grand mechanism for this transformation. "And we all, with unveiled face, beholding the glory of the Lord, are being transformed into the same image from one degree of glory to another. For this comes from the Lord who is the Spirit." Just as Moses gazed at the glory of Yahweh and his face shone, so now we behold the glory of Yahweh in Jesus Christ.[3] Paul continues just a few verses later in 2 Corinthians 4:6, "For God, who said, 'Let light shine out of darkness,' has shone in our hearts to give the light of the knowledge of the glory of God in the face of Jesus Christ."

---

[3] Heb. 1:3: "He is the radiance of the glory of God…"

The glory of God is most fully seen in the face of Jesus Christ. Only the eyes of those who have repented and believed have been opened to it. That glory is transformative, according to 2 Corinthians 3:18. Gazing at the glory of God in the face of Christ, we are transformed into the image of Christ from one degree of glory to another. Slowly, progressively, we are sanctified.

Beholding the glory of God in the face of Christ is *not* synonymous with having a cognitive awareness of the facts of the gospel. The Song of Songs is a great primer on what it means to behold the glory of God in the face of Christ. The way that the man and wife are transfixed by one another is the picture of what it means to behold the glory of Christ. To behold Christ is to be enamored with him, to be transfixed by His beauty.

How can we be transfixed by the beauty of a Savior we can't see? His beauty is not in His physical appearance, but in His character, His work, and His gospel. Meditate on the gospel. Meditate on His attributes, or excellencies, as Peter calls them.[4] Read good, rich devotional literature. For me, some modern-day authors are not as helpful as Spurgeon, Ryle, and the Puritans writing about the gospel and the beauty of Christ. When I read those old voices, the world's appeal in my heart shrivels and affection for Him steadily grows. Read the Scriptures prayerfully looking for Christ. Reading those old authors will help you learn to do that. They will help you learn to read all the Scriptures Christologically. Pray to Him for everything throughout the day, not just for a few minutes to say that you've had your quiet time. Make a priority of meeting with others to talk about Him.

Another tool that can help us to slow down and behold the glory is keeping a journal. I've never been the "Dear Diary" type, so don't worry—that's not what I'm talking about. Keeping a journal is where we force ourselves to slow down and think deeply about a passage of Scripture by writing about it. My favorite method is to read the same chapter of the Bible daily for several days so that I'm well familiar with the context and content. Each day, I will choose a verse or section and

---

[4] 1 Pet. 2:9: "But you are a chosen race, a royal priesthood, a holy nation, a people for his own possession, that you may proclaim the excellencies of him who called you out of darkness into his marvelous light."

write about it. Some days I may paraphrase the verse in my own words in four or five different ways, which makes me think hard about what it means. Other days, I may write down as many answers as I can to the question, "How is the glory of Jesus shown here?" I then write a short prayer pertaining to what I've seen in the text. This discipline, more than any other, has served to stir up my affections for the Lord over the last several years.

It's delightful to behold the glory of God in the face of Christ. As we are transfixed by it, He transforms us. The character and work of Christ seen in the Bible, when we purposefully meditate on it, causes us to want to be like Him. This desire then changes the commands of the Word from rules into gracious instruction on how to conform to His image. Seeing Him as He is makes His commands our happy choice, and we are transformed in our character and conduct.

What should be the result of our transformation into the image of Christ? Like the woman of the Song, we should not become enamored with ourselves and how we've become more holy. Rather, we should be all the more transfixed by Him. Consider Paul, who arguably became more like Jesus than any man this side of glory. What effect did Christlikeness have on his heart? He was ever more obsessed:

> But whatever gain I had, I counted as loss for the sake of Christ. Indeed, I count everything as loss because of the surpassing worth of knowing Christ Jesus my Lord. For his sake I have suffered the loss of all things and count them as rubbish, in order that I may gain Christ and be found in him, not having a righteousness of my own that comes from the law, but that which comes through faith in Christ, the righteousness from God that depends on faith—that I may know him and the power of his resurrection, and may share his sufferings, becoming like him in his death, that by any means possible I may attain the resurrection from the dead (Phil. 3:7–11).

Being like Jesus made Paul want more Jesus. "That I may attain the resurrection from the dead" is Paul's way of saying he wants to go and be with Jesus! Transformation led Paul to be all the more transfixed by the agent of his transformation, the Lord Jesus, so that he could say, "For to me to live is Christ, and to die is gain" (Phil.

1:21)! The more we become like Him, the more we want to behold the glory of God in the face of Jesus Christ. Transfixed, we are transformed, and transformed, we are transfixed.

Imitate Me as I Imitate Christ

If Christ exemplifies the love of the Song by transforming us as we are transfixed by Him, how then do we emulate that love in our marriages? Should we desire for our spouses to be transfixed by us? Not exactly. However, there is a similar idea expressed repeatedly by Paul in the New Testament: "Be imitators of me, as I am of Christ" (1 Cor. 11:1).[5]

Obviously, the apostle didn't believe that anyone would be transformed by merely being obsessed with him personally or with any other Christian, for that matter. He makes that very point in the early chapters of 1 Corinthians. We ought not idolize other believers, for no believer has the inherent power to save or sanctify others. Rather, "Let the one who boasts, boast in the Lord" (1 Cor. 1:31).

However, this does not preclude the idea that believers can serve as powerful models of Christlikeness pointing others toward the Lord. As we saw in the previous section, Paul was so enamored with Jesus and therefore transformed by Him that he wanted all those to whom he ministered to experience the same joy. Certainly, he gave detailed instructions about how to be a faithful follower of Jesus Christ, but like any good teacher, he also modeled that instruction. For this reason, numerous times we find Paul calling his readers to emulate him...as he emulated Jesus.

Because the gospel is transformative and marriage is intended to depict the gospel, as we see in the Song, our marriages should be transformative. However, they will only be so to the extent that we as husbands and wives are transfixed by Christ and not one another. Therefore, if we would love one another well, we must not only keep our own eyes on the Lord Jesus, but also do all we can to direct our spouses' attention to Him as well.

Applied to marriage, Paul's approach to ministry might look something like this: you must be transfixed by Christ not only for the

---

[5] cf 1 Cor. 4:16; Phil. 3:17; 2 Thess. 3:7

sake of your own growth, but for the sake of your spouse. Paul was very careful to live his life in such a way that he created an atmosphere that commended Jesus to those around him. This is clear in many of his letters, but perhaps nowhere more obviously than in 1 Thessalonians. It appears that the apostle was determined to encourage the faith of the believers in Thessalonica by reminding them of the example set by himself and his ministry companions. "You are witnesses, and God also, how holy and righteous and blameless was our conduct toward you believers" (1 Thess. 2:10). Yet, here is a key point—the example he set was intentional. "You know what kind of men we proved to be among you *for your sake*" (1 Thess. 1:5).

Ephesians explicitly calls us to participate in one another's sanctification:

> Husbands, love your wives, as Christ loved the church and gave himself up for her, that he might sanctify her, having cleansed her by the washing of water with the word, so that he might present the church to himself in splendor, without spot or wrinkle or any such thing, that she might be holy and without blemish. In the same way husbands should love their wives as their own bodies. He who loves his wife loves himself (Eph. 5:25–28).

1 Peter also teaches that we are to conduct ourselves with a great concern for the spiritual well-being of our spouses. Wives are to interact with their husbands in such a way that they're drawn to the Lord. Husbands are to show great care for their wives spiritually:

> Likewise, wives, be subject to your own husbands, so that even if some do not obey the word, they may be won without a word by the conduct of their wives, when they see your respectful and pure conduct. Do not let your adorning be external—the braiding of hair and the putting on of gold jewelry, or the clothing you wear—but let your adorning be the hidden person of the heart with the imperishable beauty of a gentle and quiet spirit, which in God's sight is very precious. For this is how the holy women who hoped in God used to adorn themselves, by submitting to their own husbands, as Sarah obeyed Abraham, calling him lord. And you are her children, if you do good and

do not fear anything that is frightening. Likewise, husbands, live with your wives in an understanding way, showing honor to the woman as the weaker vessel, since they are heirs with you of the grace of life, so that your prayers may not be hindered (1 Pet. 3:1–7).

A way to promote your spouse's spiritual health is to do just what Paul did. Intentionally follow and enjoy Jesus so that your spouse will see your example and be inspired to similarly follow and enjoy Him. Your life will say to your spouse, "Imitate me as I imitate Jesus." The joy that you exhibit in your walk with Him will likely be infectious.

Every Christian husband and Christian wife have a Christ-appointed 24/7 sanctification training partner. The vast majority of influences in this world, including our own flesh, prod us to take from our spouses, place expectations upon them, and look for how they're going to benefit us. Certainly, we need our spouses, but the Scriptures call us to pour ourselves out for them—that they might be transformed into the image of Christ. A premier way to do this is to be transfixed by Jesus, in a constant process of transformation into His likeness, so that the road of discipleship is commended to this person with whom you've made a lifelong covenant before the Lord.

As a husband and wife are both transfixed by Christ, both transformed into His image, and therefore increasingly loving one another as He does the church, their marriage will point to something greater than themselves. Their marriage will be a spectacle that transfixes a watching world and commends the gospel. Although our marriages should be beautiful by the transforming power of the Lord Jesus Christ, the enjoyable beauty of marriage should not be regarded as an end in itself, but as a means to glory in the agent of its transformation.

Discussion Questions/Activities

1. When thinking about gospel themes, do you tend to struggle to think of transformation, or sanctification, as part of the ongoing work of Christ? Why or why not? What biblical texts should guide our thinking on these things?

2. As we grow in Christlikeness, why does it make no sense to grow in pride about our transformation? If we are like the woman of the Song, where will our focus turn as we are increasingly transformed?

3. "Beholding the glory of God in the face of Christ is *not* synonymous with having a cognitive awareness of the facts of the gospel." What are three practical disciplines you can practice to behold the glory God in the face of Christ? Do you see the glory of Jesus' character, works, and gospel in these three?

4. Have you ever considered that your being transfixed and transformed could be a means of spurring on your spouse to greater enjoyment of the Lord? Discuss with your spouse how you each are doing in your walk with the Lord. How is your walk affecting your spouse and vice-versa?

12

BORNE & BOUND

A Tale of Two Robertsons

In 2011, Pat Robertson famously declared that it was permissible to divorce a spouse suffering with Alzheimer's.[1] The televangelist shared that he could not fault a man for desiring companionship, but he advised that one should make sure custodial care was in place. It's sad when the world's ideal of imminently quenchable love becomes the basis for religious marriage counsel, even among the marginally biblical.

However, consider a Robertson who embodied a higher ideal of love—*the very flame of Yahweh*. Robertson McQuilkin met his wife Muriel while they were both students at Columbia Bible College and Seminary. They enjoyed a vibrant life together as educators and missionaries, raising six children together. Eventually both worked at Columbia, where Robertson became the president in 1968.

However, in the 1980's after over four decades of marriage, Robertson began to notice changes in Muriel's personality and memory. She was soon diagnosed with Alzheimer's disease. Friends and colleagues encouraged Robertson to put Muriel in an institution

---

[1] Ravelle Mohammed, "Pat Robertson Blasted for Alzheimer's Divorce Advice," *The Christian Post*, September 14, 2011, sec. Church & Ministries, https://www.christianpost.com/news/pat-robertson-blasted-for-alzheimers-divorce-advice.html.

where she could receive professional care, while he continued his work for Columbia. Instead, at the peak of his career in 1990, he resigned to care for Muriel full-time. His touching resignation speech has become somewhat famous. Below is an excerpt:

> I haven't in my life experienced easy decision-making on major decisions, but one of the simplest and clearest decisions I've had to make is this one because circumstances dictated it. Muriel now, in the last couple of months, seems to be almost happy when with me and almost never happy when not with me. In fact, she seems to feel trapped, becomes very fearful, sometimes almost terror, and when she can't get to me there can be anger. She's in distress. But when I'm with her she's happy and contented, and so I must be with her at all times.
>
> And you see, it's not only that I promised in sickness and in health, 'till death do us part, and I'm a man of my word. But as I have said…it's the only fair thing. She sacrificed for me for forty years to make my life possible. So if I cared for her for forty years, I'd still be in debt.
>
> However, there's much more. It's not that I *have* to. It's that I *get* to. I love her very dearly, and you can tell it's not easy to talk about. She's a delight. And it's a great honor to care for such a wonderful person.[2]

Due to how advanced the disease was at the time, it was reasonable to assume that Robertson would be caring full-time for Muriel for only a few months or years. However, due largely to his loving care, Muriel lived another 13 years before dying at age 81. Upon her death, and though advanced in age himself, Robertson returned to a speaking and writing ministry.

Regarding Pat Robertson's ill-advised counsel, Ed Stetzer wrote,

> Not only was Robertson McQuilkin like Jesus in keeping his word to Muriel; he was like Jesus in his love for her…this is how Christ's love for the church is our model—he laid down

---

[2] Sarah Eekhoff Zylstra, "Died: Robertson McQuilkin, College President Praised for Alzheimer's Resignation," *Christianity Today*, June 2, 2016, https://www.christianitytoday.com/news/2016/june/died-robertson-mcquilkin-columbia-president-alzheimers-ciu.html.

his life. So should we. When it comes to marriage and Alzheimer's, listen to Robertson McQuilken and not Pat Robertson.[3]

The love depicted in the Song of Songs is a love extraordinarily powerful that cannot be quenched. It binds two people together physically, emotionally, and spiritually. It makes a commitment not merely to stay together, but to love fiercely until death. Praise God for godly husbands and wives like Robertson and Muriel McQuilkin who remind us that there is a love available to us from above that cannot be taken down by earthly troubles. *Its flashes are flashes of fire, the very flame of the LORD* (Song 8:6).

The Song (8:5–7)

(Chorus)

> 5 *Who is that coming up from the wilderness, leaning on her beloved?*

(She)

> *Under the apple tree I awakened you. There your mother was in labor with you; there she who bore you was in labor.*
>
> 6 *Set me as a seal upon your heart, as a seal upon your arm, for love is strong as death, jealousy is fierce as the grave. Its flashes are flashes of fire, the very flame of the LORD.*
>
> 7 *Many waters cannot quench love, neither can floods drown it. If a man offered for love all the wealth of his house, he would be utterly despised.*

Most interpreters view this passage as something of a climax, which is interesting in that it is possibly the least sexual passage in the Song. It's a climax in that the previous chapters lead the woman here to make both a critical request of her husband and a grand statement

---

[3] Ed Stetzer, "On Marriage and Alzheimer's Disease: Listen to Robertson McQuilkin and Not Pat Robertson," *Christianity Today*, September 15, 2011, sec. Culture, Leadership, https://www.christianitytoday.com/edstetzer/2011/september/on-marriage-and-alzheimers-disease-listen-to-robertson.html.

about love itself. It contains some of the most beautiful verses in the Bible, tying marital love directly to the heart of God.

The passage begins with the voice of the chorus: "Who is that coming up from the wilderness..." (8:5). These are nearly the same words as 3:6, where the object was the bride of Solomon, being carried on his litter. By using this question again, the author—Solomon—is once again making a contrast. While the nameless, numberless bride of chapter 3 was being carried by a somewhat impersonal fanfare to a marriage that would be anything but monogamous, meaningful, and truly intimate, the bride of the Song is being borne by her husband himself. She is being borne up by *him*. It's a picture of intimate dependence.

According to the rest of verse 5, that intimate dependence is mutual. She speaks: "Under the apple tree I awakened you. There your mother was in labor with you; there she who bore you was in labor." Our attention should be called back to chapter 2 where the woman likened her husband to an apple tree in the forest. He was an apple tree whose fruit was sweet to her taste. In that scene in 2:6, she said, "His left hand is under my head, and his right hand embraces me." Then for the first time in the Song she exhorted the daughters of Jerusalem, "Don't stir up or awaken love until it pleases. Don't do what we're doing until it's time." Here in chapter 8, she's calling her husband's attention back to that scene, saying, "I awakened you." "Awakened"—that's the same verb she uses in her exhortation to the daughters of Jerusalem. The marital love that she gave to her husband awakened him.

Of the tree in chapter 2, she says, "That's where your mother was in labor with you; that's where she gave birth to you." There's a comparison taking place. "Your mother gave birth to you there, but I awakened you there. You really came to life when we were joined together."

This reminds me of a great country song. I'll give you just a few lines.

I was born the day you kissed me
I died inside the night you left me

But I lived, oh how I lived while you loved me.[4]

There seems to be an unwritten rule in the Nashville songwriting community that something like 70% of love songs must involve someone leaving someone else. However, if you take that middle line out– "I died inside the night you left me," you're left with: "I was born the day you kissed me...I lived, oh how I lived while you loved me." Those lyrics say something very similar to what the woman is communicating in verse 5: "You were really born the day I kissed you; you really began to live when we began to love one another. Your mom gave birth to you, but I awakened you."

This means that the man is as dependent on the woman as she is on him. He is more profoundly connected to and dependent upon her than he is to his mother. She rests on him; he was wakened by her. They're connected in mutual dependence.

All this leads her to say in verse 6, "Set me as a seal upon your heart, as a seal upon your arm..." In the ancient world, a person's seal was often like a signet ring. It bore their unique mark, which was like a signature. On an official document, that ring would be used like a stamp to authenticate the identity of the signer. Sometimes it would be used to seal a letter. It could also be used to place a mark of ownership on a possession. It was a statement and guarantee of that person's identity. To engrave your unique mark on a signet ring was in a sense to engrave your identity on that ring.

Moreover, you wouldn't leave it lying around. It was a highly prized possession. Some people would wear that ring around their neck or tie it on an arm, so that it was secure, close to them at all times. Therefore, some commentators hold that the woman is saying, "Let me stamp my seal on you." In other words, "Make it obvious to everyone that I own you, heart and body." However, the text indicates she wants to be the actual signet ring. If you look at the other places this noun is used in the Old Testament, it refers to the ring itself, not the mark it makes. One of those texts, the last verse of Haggai (2:23), uses the same verb and noun. There in Haggai, the Lord says to Zerubbabel, "I will take you...and make you like a signet ring, for I

---

[4] From "While You Loved Me," originally recorded by Rascal Flatts. Written by Kim Williams, Danny Wells, and Marty Dodson.

have chosen you." This is the same verb and object, and the idea is that Zerubbabel will *be* Yahweh's signet ring.

The woman doesn't want to be a mark on his arm and heart, expressing her ownership of him. She wants to be his signet ring. Of course, this is figurative language. What she means is, "Engrave your identity on me." That's what you do with a signet ring. "Engrave your identity on me. Make me part of who you are."

"On your heart and on your arm," simply conveys, "Hold me as close as possible, not just physically, but also to your heart. Cherish me. Bind me inextricably to yourself. Make me essential to your life. Make me part of you and make this permanent."

She goes on in verse 6 to justify this request by commenting on the nature of love itself: "…for love is strong as death, jealousy is fierce as the grave. Its flashes are flashes of fire, the very flame of the LORD." Those first two lines— "Love is strong as death, jealousy is fierce as the grave"—are saying the same thing. Each of the three main words in each clause should be considered close synonyms—love and jealousy, strong and fierce, and death and the grave.

We tend to think of jealousy as a negative thing, but it is not inherently so. Jealousy is simply a reluctance or refusal to share something that belongs to you. If that thing is something that should only belong to you or should only be enjoyed by you, jealousy is a good thing. If that thing is something intended to be shared, jealousy is a bad thing. I should not be jealous of my time, money, food, or other resources. However, when it comes to the romantic love of my wife, it is appropriate for me to be jealous. That is, it is appropriate for me to refuse to share her romantic love with anyone else. By God's design, it belongs exclusively to me. In fact, for me to share it with anyone else would be an abomination to God.

By making "love" parallel to "jealousy" in these two lines, the author is showing that godly marital love is a jealous love. It wants exclusivity. It wants permanent attachment. It does not want to share what God has designed not to be shared. So we might initially read her request to be his signet ring—that is, to be essential to him—and think, "That's awfully possessive." No, this is the nature of love itself. The close physical, emotional, and spiritual intimacy between a man and wife should be exclusive. That is the nature of marital love.

As the woman says here, this godly jealousy/love is strong as death, fierce as the grave. What should we make of that statement? Well, can death be denied? Have any of us ever known someone to negotiate with death and win? Certainly not. When death comes for you, it wins the day. We're speaking in human terms. Of course, God has power over death. However, from our perspective, when death comes, it cannot be denied. Death is relentless in the sense that it gets what it wants. When your time comes, your time comes.

Likewise, this godly jealousy of marital love cannot be negotiated. It is righteously territorial, and it will not be denied. Just as death will not loosen its grip when the time comes, so also marital love will not loosen its exclusive claim to the one loved. *My beloved is mine and I am His.*

She goes on to describe this love as flashes of fire—the very flame of Yahweh. Whenever we talk about jealous love, we should automatically think of our great God. In Exodus 34:14, God says of Himself, "The LORD, whose name is Jealous, is a jealous God."[5] In the Ten Commandments of Exodus 20, as the first two commands are given— "You shall have no other gods before me," and "You shall not make for yourself a carved image," the reason given is this: "For I the LORD your God am a jealous God" (Exo. 20:2–5). God will not share with another what belongs exclusively to Him. The worship, affection, and adoration of His people is His alone; He will not share it with another god. This is a righteous disposition, an aspect of His love for His people.

Related, Deuteronomy 4:24 forbids false worship, saying, "For the LORD your God is a consuming fire, a jealous God." We tend to associate the flame of God with judgment, which is appropriate. Yet, it is also a function of His love to ferociously protect the exclusivity of His relationship with His people. The desire of the woman in the Song to hold her husband close to herself, to be held close to him, to claim him as her own, and to call him to absolute fidelity reflects the flame of Yahweh, the righteously jealous love of God.

She goes on to describe just how strong it is in verse 7: "Many waters cannot quench love, neither can floods drown it." You and I

---

[5] In the ESV and most other major translations, "LORD" in all capital letters represents "Yahweh" in the underlying Hebrew text.

have never seen a fire that can't be quenched. Every fire that has ever existed on this earth was quenchable. Get enough water and you can put out any fire. However, the love described here is the very flame of Yahweh. There is not enough water to put out that fire. Godly love cannot be extinguished.

The rest of the verse speaks to how invaluable love is: "If a man offered for love all the wealth of his house, he would be utterly despised." This righteously jealous love is so valuable that if Jeff Bezos, who is worth over $100 billion, offered all his wealth for it, the offer would be so insultingly low he would be despised for it. This kind of godly love is so valuable…well, it's invaluable.

Christ, The Jealous

Just as the woman desires to be the signet ring of her husband, so we should desire to bear Christ's image upon ourselves. He desires for us to be His signet ring, so to speak, that we might reflect who He is. We are conformed to His image as we hold tightly to Him, loving Him above all. This fierce, righteously jealous love is what Christ desires from us. It is an ultimate allegiance. No one and nothing comes before Him, for our hearts are bound only to Him.

Jesus said to His disciples in Matthew 10:35–38,

> For I have come to set a man against his father, and a daughter against her mother, and a daughter-in-law against her mother-in-law. And a person's enemies will be those of his own household. Whoever loves father or mother more than me is not worthy of me, and whoever loves son or daughter more than me is not worthy of me. And whoever does not take his cross and follow me is not worthy of me.

To follow Christ is to live for Him alone, to love Him above all, and to worship Him alone. This is not *super* discipleship. It is discipleship.

However, we have a problem, which is exposed in the Bible through the history of Israel. God is a God of fiercely jealous love, who expected absolute, permanent monogamy from His people. Yet, His people had hearts prone to wander. Almost immediately upon being redeemed from Egypt, the Israelites showed unfaithfulness to Yahweh. They did not trust Him. They chased after false gods.

The heart of the problem was revealed in startling fashion in Joshua 24. After repeated calls to be faithful to Yahweh, Joshua called on the people to renew their covenant with him, saying, "Choose this day whom you will serve, whether the gods your fathers served in the region beyond the River, or the gods of the Amorites in whose land you dwell. But as for me and my house, we will serve the LORD (Jos. 24:15)." The people replied with a hearty, "Yes, we'll serve the Lord, too." However, Joshua's response in 24:19 was shocking: "You are not able to serve the LORD, for he is a holy God. He is a jealous God; he will not forgive your transgressions or your sins. If you forsake the LORD and serve foreign gods, then he will turn and do you harm and consume you, after having done you good."

The book of Judges shows that Joshua was exactly right. The people were unable to remain faithful to the Lord. They repeatedly went back to their false worship in spite of the judgment it brought upon them. The people needed new hearts. They needed to be changed from the inside out. So characteristic was this spiritual adultery that the prophets Jeremiah and Malachi referred to the people of God repeatedly as "faithless Israel," playing the whore after every god on every high hill (Jer. 3:11; Mal. 2:11).

The Israelites were not unique. Their condition is the condition of all men. God requires the exclusive worship and adoration of all people, yet none are capable. We should see in the history of Israel that it was not a unique history, but a commentary on our own hearts.

Graciously, the prophet Zechariah offers a beautiful word, an answer to the problem of "faithless Israel." In his eighth chapter, Zechariah writes, "Thus says the LORD of hosts: I am jealous for Zion with great jealousy, and I am jealous for her with great wrath. Thus says the LORD: I have returned to Zion and will dwell in the midst of Jerusalem, and Jerusalem shall be called *the faithful city*..." (Zec. 8:2–3).

When we read of Jerusalem, Israel, and Judah in the Old Testament, those promises are not exclusive to an ethnic group. They are ours by faith, according to Galatians 3:29.[6] That the Lord will dwell in the midst of Jerusalem could be a reference to the new heavens and new earth, but it is foundationally the new covenant in

---

[6] Gal. 3:29: And if you are Christ's, then you are Abraham's offspring, heirs according to promise.

Christ's blood, inaugurated at the Lord's Supper. He lives in our midst through His Spirit who dwells within us. For Jerusalem to be called "the faithful city" is parallel to the promises in Jeremiah 31:31–34 and Ezekiel 36:26 that He gives a new heart. He makes us faithful. He puts a new Spirit inside of us. He turns the faithless into the faithful. What a relief! What good news!

This godly, jealous, monogamous love that God has for His people and which Jesus requires of His disciples, He enables in His disciples. He changes us so that we are characterized by faithfulness to Him. He keeps us faithful![7] 1 Peter 1:3–5 teaches, "According to his great mercy, he has caused us to be born again to a living hope through the resurrection of Jesus Christ from the dead, to an inheritance that is imperishable, undefiled, and unfading, kept in heaven for you, who by God's power are being guarded through faith for a salvation ready to be revealed in the last time." Our inheritance is being kept in heaven for us, and He is keeping us by His power through faith.

This woman of the Song says to her husband, "Be faithful to me. Be as fiercely jealous as I am." This is the nature of godly marital love. This is what God intended. We in our natural state are not capable of such a thing. Jesus says the same thing to us, echoing the Old Testament, "Be faithful to me, worship no one else, be as fiercely jealous as I am."

Here is the wonder of it all: He *died* to pay the penalty for our former unfaithfulness and to give us new hearts, faithful hearts. By the Spirit who dwells inside us, He *keeps* us in the faith. He keeps us faithful to Him. He jealously holds us fast so that we do not let go of Him. His unquenchable love binds us to Him in so profound a way that the only way for the New Testament authors to describe it is with phrases like "you are in Christ," and "Christ in us." Not on us. Not beside us. In us. We are in Him.

If ever your heart has cried out to Him, if ever you have desired Him, if ever you have believed, if ever you have found Him beautiful—get on your knees and praise Him—He worked that in you!

---

[7] The means He uses to keep us faithful are beyond the scope of this section. In other words, I'm not attempting to describe how He keeps us faithful; I'm just establishing that He does.

By nature, we're rebels. He rescued us from our own hearts! He makes us faithful.

For this faithfulness, we are dependent upon Him. He bears us up. We depend not upon our own will power, but the power of the Holy Spirit. I'm reminded of Matthew 11:28–30—His call to us in our lostness, restlessness, and fruitless labor, a call that is still music to us on this side of the cross: "Come to me, all who labor and are heavy laden, and I will give you rest. Take my yoke upon you, and learn from me, for I am gentle and lowly in heart, and you will find rest for your souls. For my yoke is easy, and my burden is light." Jesus bears us up and binds us to Himself.

A Higher, Grander Command

This is the very flame of Yahweh...

What a tremendous privilege to participate in a love that brings such glory to the God who saved us. When we follow Christ by exhibiting this fiercely loyal, fiercely jealous, godly love for our spouses, we experience marital love as it was intended, and we shine the very flame of Yahweh to the world. This is simply another way of describing the text we've returned to so many times in Ephesians 5:22–33. By embracing God's design, we experience the divine on the human plane and we commend the gospel to those around us.

This climactic passage in the Song should make us shoot for the stars, as it were. It should inspire us to believe in the power of God to do amazing things in us for His glory. He can foster in husbands and wives a love that binds them together emotionally, spiritually, and physically so that they, like the woman of the Song, live a love that says, "Set me as a seal upon your heart, as a seal upon your arm, for love is strong as death, jealousy is fierce as the grave" (8:6).

Sadly, many husbands and wives injured by years of hurts and plagued by a low view of the gospel have a far lower trajectory for their marriages. Their goal is to simply stay married. Rather than being bound emotionally, spiritually, and physically, they are merely aiming to remain bound legally. I've heard people say things like, "I'm staying married strictly out of obedience. I know it's unlawful to divorce so I'm staying with my spouse to honor God." Then that broken, loveless marriage is where they settle, live, and mark time.

What a travesty if we were to believe that the application of such a glorious text were, "Don't get a divorce." If you're staying married because you want to glorify God, that is commendable. However, I want you to consider something. Your legally intact, but loveless marriage may be more harmful to the gospel than a divorce would be.

Don't misunderstand. I am not saying if you can't love each other with the ideal love of the Song, you should end it. No, the answer to one sin isn't another sin. Rather, the answer is to repent of your loveless marriage and obey *all* that the Scriptures teach about marriage. There are commands in the Bible pertaining to marriage that are higher and grander than the prohibition against divorce. How can we obey only the most obvious and fundamental command and say that we've honored the Lord? Believing that we've fulfilled our obligation to God in marriage as long as we don't get a divorce is like thinking that as long as we don't kill our children we've fulfilled our obligation to God in our parenting.

Just staying married and calling it a day is a gross lowering of the bar. Ephesians 5:22–28 calls husbands to love their wives as Christ loved the church; it commands wives to submit to and respect their husbands as the church does Christ. Of course, stay married, but merely staying married is well shy of what God expects of us as spouses. A broken, but legally intact marriage is not a faithful picture of the gospel.

Stop thinking of "no divorce" as the bare minimum. Christlike love is the bare minimum. Without advocating divorce, I want to open your eyes to how damaging a loveless marriage is to the gospel message. A divorce says to the world, "Something obviously went wrong here. This isn't how it's supposed to be. This one failed." A legally-intact, but loveless Christian marriage lies about the gospel by saying, "Yes, this is what love is supposed to be. This is normal. This is how Christ loves the church and the church responds to Christ." Perish the thought! We should hate divorce with a passion—it should grieve us. However, where is the remorse, where is the grief over our rampant disregard for higher commands pertaining to marriage?

Many people have the mindset, "I want to avoid divorce at all costs because it would dishonor God." That's true, but let's raise the bar to where Scripture has it. We should have the mindset, "I would rather die than defame the gospel with a *loveless* marriage. I repent of this." Therefore, the application is much more than simply staying legally bound to this person that you married however many years ago. The love that Yahweh has for His people, the love that Christ has for His church—this is the love we are to have for our spouses. "Set me as a seal on your heart, as a seal on your arm" (8:6). Exhibit toward your spouse this fiercely exclusive, righteously jealous love.

"Many waters cannot quench love, neither can floods drown it" (8:9). This is the nature of godly love. Nothing could quench the love of Christ for His bride. The same should be true of us if we would emulate Him. Have a heart toward your spouse that says, "There is nothing you can do to cause me to stop loving you or to cause me to stop wanting you for myself alone." Exhibit a marriage in which you are not simply bound by the law of the land, but instead knitted together physically, emotionally, and spiritually by a love that can only come from God Himself, where you're faithful to one another not simply with your body, but with your mind and your heart. Consider yourself bound, not by shackles, but by godly love that cannot be extinguished—the very flame of Yahweh. Just read the Song. This is love and affection. This is godly marital love. This is what commends the gospel to a watching world.

Discussion Questions/Activities

1. Why is it good for God to be a jealous God? What does His jealousy teach us about godly, marital love?

2. Recall the days prior to your conversion. In what ways did your life reflect the marks of "faithless Israel"? What differences do you see in your life now that Christ has changed you and bound you to Himself?

3. Have you been guilty of lowering the bar as it pertains to honoring God with your marriage by just remaining married? What effects has this had on the quality of your marriage?

4. If the Bible is true, what prevents you from loving your spouse like Christ loves the church? How can Christ change everything?

13

FULLNESS & FREEDOM

Fire Safety

Any survival expert can recommend a list of essential skills that every person should acquire if they expect to make it through a garden-variety emergency. One such skill is ironic in that it is necessary for survival in many situations, and yet the improper handling of it can be deadlier than not having it at all. It's the ability to make fire.

All the lifesaving benefits of fire, such as signaling for help, boiling water, and cooking food, require that it be built and maintained within appropriate boundaries. A typical suggestion is that the fire be built at least six feet away from any trees, within a circle of large rocks to serve as a barrier to keep the fire from spreading. Dry, easily combustible materials must be carefully removed from close proximity to the fire prior to starting it. Without these boundaries, one survival situation can quickly turn into a worse one.

In October 2003, a hunter was separated from his friend and became lost in the Cleveland National Forest of southern California. After wandering for hours, the dehydrated and disoriented man decided to light a signal fire. In a near panic, *he then hastily lit a second one*. That was at 5:35pm. Three minutes later, the first of many 911 calls were made reporting the blaze.[1]

---

[1] Dave Downey, "Firestorm 2003: The Story of a Catastrophe," *The San Diego Union-Tribune*, November 16, 2003, https://www.sandiegouniontribune.com/sdut-firestorm-2003-the-story-of-a-catastrophe-2003nov16-story.html.

The dry autumn season of San Diego County created ideal conditions for a fast-moving wildfire. What would come to be called the Cedar Fire traveled 28 miles in the first 14 hours. It eventually joined another blaze dubbed the Paradise fire, which was ignited of unknown cause near Valley Center. Over the course of 11 days, the two fires devoured a patch of real estate larger than Los Angeles. Three hundred thousand acres and 2,400 homes were destroyed. Sixteen people were killed.[2] It was the largest wildfire in California history.

It is for good reason that the woman of the Song has likened love—emotional, spiritual, sexual love—to a fire: "For love is strong as death, jealousy is fierce as the grave. Its flashes are flashes of fire, the very flame of the LORD. Many waters cannot quench love, neither can floods drown it" (8:6–7). That unquenchable fire in the appropriate context is sublime. At times, it even seems life-giving. However, apart from the appropriate boundaries, it is absolutely devastating.

If love is an unquenchable fire, marriage is the safe environment that God created for the enjoyment of that fire. Yet, the rebellious human heart wants what it wants on its own terms, without boundaries. What God has created to be an environment of safety is regarded by many to stifle freedom and fullness. Looking for sexual fulfillment outside of marriage, they think they want for a good thing. In the end they are like fools who would burn down the world for the sake of their desperation.

As the Song has taught us, in its proper context, God's good gift of marital sexual love is explosively pleasurable…and safe. Holding God's gifts in the proper context is the only way to enjoy them with freedom and fullness. The woman of the Song with her refrain, "I adjure you…that you not stir up or awaken love until it pleases," has been communicating that message (2:7, 3:5, 8:4). With these final verses, we see again the admonition to keep God's good gift where He has designed it to be enjoyed. Loss comes from disregarding this; fullness and freedom come from embracing it.

---

[2] Tony Perry, "35-Year-Old Sentenced in Deadly Cedar Fire," *Los Angeles Times*, November 18, 2005, https://www.latimes.com/archives/la-xpm-2005-nov-18-me-cedar18-story.html.

The Song (8:8–14)

(Chorus)

*8 We have a little sister, and she has no breasts. What shall we do
for our sister on the day when she is spoken for?*

*9 If she is a wall, we will build on her a battlement of silver, but if
she is a door, we will enclose her with boards of cedar.*

(She)

*10 I was a wall, and my breasts were like towers; then I was in
his eyes as one who finds peace.*

*11 Solomon had a vineyard at Baal-hamon; he let out the vineyard
to keepers; each one was to bring for its fruit a thousand pieces
of silver.*

*12 My vineyard, my very own, is before me; you, O Solomon, may
have the thousand, and the keepers of the fruit two hundred.*

(He)

*13 O you who dwell in the gardens, with companions listening for
your voice; let me hear it.*

(She)

*14 Make haste, my beloved, and be like a gazelle or a young stag
on the mountains of spices.*

The chorus begins this final passage in verse 8, "We have a little
sister, and she has no breasts. What shall we do for our sister on the
day when she is spoken for?" The comment about her body just means
that she's a little girl. More importantly, they want to know what they
should do to prepare their little sister for betrothal.

It seems they are consulting among themselves in verse 9: "If she
is a wall, we will build on her a battlement of silver, but if she is a door,
we will enclose her with boards of cedar." Consider the difference
between a wall and a door. A wall keeps out, while a door lets in. Being
a wall means that she's committed to remaining a virgin until marriage.
No one is getting through the wall. Being a door means that she is
permissive, willing to let someone in. That is, she's not so committed
to remaining a virgin. So, if she is a wall, committed to purity, they will

support her resolve by placing a silver fortification on her. If she's a door, they will barricade her with cedar planks. In other words, if she is promiscuous, they will make her into a wall. They will do everything they can to prevent her from losing her virginity, whether she likes it or not.

They are committed to seeing their little sister to marriage with her virginity intact. This is a good thing. They are taking to heart the woman's refrain in the Song, "I adjure you...that you not stir up or awaken love until it pleases" (8:4). We could assume that they have adopted this resolve themselves, and now they want to help their little sister down the same road.

The imagery used here is that of a fortress. There is a force trying to conquer her virginity. That force could be males wanting her before her time, but it could also be her own sexual desire. At any rate, the struggle is described in terms of a military engagement. These people are determined to help their little sister fight the war.

The woman of the Song comments in verse 10: "I was a wall, and my breasts were like towers; then I was in his eyes as one who finds peace." The woman of the Song is giving her own testimony. Of course, what stands out in the first half of the verse is her comment about her breasts. Her point is that she wasn't just a wall when she was a little girl; she was a wall when she was fully developed. The word "towers" speaks not merely to the size of her anatomy, but to the fortification of the wall—her zeal for chastity. Towers on a wall were the most important part of a defense. She did exactly what she told the daughters of Jerusalem to do. She didn't stir up or awaken love until it pleased. She remained strong until the appropriate time.

Then she became in his eyes as one who finds peace. This idea of peace plays on the military metaphors already used. Being a wall, she withstood the bombardment of temptation. Yet, now her king, as she described him in chapter 1, has penetrated the wall by her invitation, and his banner over her is love (2:4). His presence and love have brought peace—the cessation of resistance to sexual desire. She held out until the appropriate time and context. Then with her husband alone, she found the end of resisting, the end of putting up her guard. She waited to taste love until inside the bonds of marriage, and therefore, she found peace.

The woman begins to comment on the great value of this peace in verse 11: "Solomon had a vineyard at Baal-hamon; he let out the vineyard to keepers; each one was to bring for its fruit a thousand pieces of silver." At first glance, it may seem that this scene has nothing to do with the previous scene in which the others asked the question, "What shall we do for our younger sister on the day when she is spoken for?" Yet, there is a connection. Solomon, the author of the Song, repeatedly presents himself as a foil for the love of the man and woman. The question by the others and the woman's response give her the opportunity to demonstrate that she has done things the right way. Conversely, the statement about Solomon shows that he has done things the wrong way. He stirred up love outside of God's prescribed context. His love life demonstrates that worldly excesses in the area of sexual love will rob one of the potent joy of God's ideal.

"Solomon had a vineyard at Baal-Hamon." Baal-hamon is not an actual place, but rather a made-up location that could be literally translated, "Husband of a crowd." Most commentators believe that the name of this vineyard indicates what it represents, which is Solomon's harem. Solomon had a vast collection of women—1,000, according to 1 Kings 11:3. This picture of keepers tending his vineyard for him shows that Solomon's love life, if you could call it that, is characterized by unnatural distance from the source of his sexual pleasure. There is no genuine intimacy, the joining of two whole persons in a one-flesh relationship. He does not know the love so enjoyed by this husband and wife. He has only ever known impersonal, commercial love.

The wisdom of the world would say that Solomon had all the sexual pleasure anyone could ever wish for—real sexual freedom, unencumbered by the confines of God's restrictions. However, Solomon's own point is that he has had nothing like the fullness and freedom of the man and woman of the Song.

This is exactly the point of verse 12. The woman says: "My vineyard, my very own, is before me; you, O Solomon, may have the thousand, and the keepers of the fruit two hundred." This calls our attention back to chapter 1, where the woman said of her brothers that they kept her busy with other vineyards, and she had no time to care for her own vineyard. As the Song progressed, the vineyard came to represent the sexuality between her and her husband. The point here is that she has her own vineyard right in front of her. She knows intimacy that Solomon can never know. She's saying to Solomon, "You can have your opulent, impersonal harem. I want the love depicted in this Song. My beloved is mine, and I am his." Solomon, the author of the Song, is making the point, through the words of the woman, "She has, within the parameters of God's good design, something far better than I have."

The goodness of God's boundaries is felt in verses 13–14, the final verses of the Song: "O you who dwell in the gardens, with companions listening for your voice; let me hear it. Make haste, my beloved, and be like a gazelle or a young stag on the mountains of spices." Verse 13 is voiced by the husband. He is saying to her, "You have companions listening for your voice, a crowd admiring you." In this, she mirrors him at the beginning of the Song. We're reminded of how his love has transformed her, how she has become complete because of their union. She has not been shackled by God's design, but she has been freed by it. Her husband himself is one of her admirers. Here he seems to echo his own words in 2:14, "Let me hear your voice, for your voice is sweet."

She answers in verse 14 with words taken from chapter 2. If you remember the passage about the gazelle on the mountains of spices from chapter 2, you know that she is inviting him to sexual intimacy once again. Therefore, he wants to hear her voice; she wants to give him her body.

This may seem like a strange way to end the Song. It's like no conclusion at all, as if the story got cut off in the middle. Perhaps, that is the point. This is a song, and there is at the end something like a repeat sign taking us back to chapter 2: they enjoy the good gift of marriage over and over. In the context of divine, marital love, they have gained freedom—freedom to give of themselves and receive of one another perpetually. God's good gifts can only be enjoyed with fullness and freedom in the context for which He created them.

Christ, Our Emancipator

The devil's original lie was that fulfillment comes from throwing off the moral constraints of God; if we want to know fullness and freedom, we must take them for ourselves. The lie echoes all around us all the time. It is no less a lie today, and yet it is embraced by the world without question.

In Genesis 2, God gave man a law for his own good: "You may surely eat of every tree of the garden, but of the tree of the knowledge of good and evil you shall not eat, for in the day that you eat of it you shall surely die" (Gen. 2:16–17). God gave a framework, and within this framework man was free to enjoy endless pleasures. However, if he stepped out of this framework, there would be death. It didn't take long for the enemy to bring his lie to bear.

> [The serpent] said to the woman, 'Did God actually say, "You shall not eat of any tree in the garden"?' And the woman said to the serpent, 'We may eat of the fruit of the trees in the garden, but God said, "You shall not eat of the fruit of the tree that is in the midst of the garden, neither shall you touch it, lest you die."' But the serpent said to the woman, 'You will not surely die. For God knows that when you eat of it your eyes will be opened, and you will be like God, knowing good and evil' (Gen 3:1–5).

God said essentially, "If you go outside of My framework, it will be death for you." The devil said, "This isn't going to be bad for you; it will be good for you. God is withholding joy." The reality was that God was protecting man. All God's laws are protective. However, the man and the woman didn't trust God. Instead, they trusted the devil, plunging themselves and all creation into darkness. Now all mankind is born believing the same lie that says, "When God tells you that you can't have something, He's keeping something good from you. God's laws are restrictive and malevolent." The devil promised freedom, but he delivered slavery. Man became enslaved to sin and death, and he lost the freedom and fullness of God's presence and good gifts—just as God had said.

All people naturally, habitually trade God's truth for the devil's lie, and for their betrayal deserve eternal banishment in hell. Yet, God promised right there in Genesis 3:15 that He would provide a solution: the seed of the woman would bruise the head of the serpent. Hebrews 2:14 teaches, "[Jesus] likewise partook of [flesh and blood], that through death he might destroy the one who has the power of death, that is, the devil, and deliver all those who through fear of death were subject to lifelong slavery." Jesus came to bring us back to fullness and freedom.

"Truly, truly, I say to you, everyone who practices sin is a slave to sin. The slave does not remain in the house forever; the son remains forever. So if the Son sets you free, you will be free indeed" (John 8:34–36). To remove the curse of sin, Jesus took that curse upon Himself, and died on the cross in our place. All those who repent and trust in Him have His perfect record imputed to their account and their sins forgiven. In Christ, they are free—free to enjoy the fullness of God and His good gifts in the context for which He created them. By believing the devil's lies, we lost the fullness of God and the freedom of fellowship with Him. By faith, we are restored to it in Christ.

Embattled Boundaries

There is pertinent application of these things to those who may be struggling to respect the context for God's good gift of sexuality. The world and our flesh echo the voice of the serpent, saying, "Has God really said that sexuality is only to be enjoyed inside the bounds of marriage? Stop denying yourself what will make you happy." He attacks with a vengeance those who live in loveless marriages, seeking to convince them that time is running out if they would know the love they've always desired. He preys on those struggling with same-sex attraction, telling them that their heterosexual marriages could never have fulfilled them. He exerts tremendous pressure on the unmarried chaste, making them a pariah class. To all, he preaches that they must throw off the constraints of archaic biblical interpretations and think about themselves for once. He has largely been successful. The world has swallowed the lie that fullness and freedom can be found outside of God's design. According to the culture, you *must* have sex outside of His design in order to enjoy the fullness of life and to be free.

Premarital sex is the cultural norm. If you are not married in this culture and you are committed to remaining a virgin before marriage, you will be regarded with a level of suspicion formerly reserved only for sexual deviants. In fact, a commitment to virginity before marriage is regarded by our culture as a form of sexual deviance. Extramarital sex is also commonplace. A cottage industry of online services has popped up offering adultery to anyone willing to make a profile. One such site—the motto of which is "Life is short. Have an affair."— boasted *60 million users* as of February 2019. Some of us work in environments where adultery is absolutely rampant. I have a friend who says that in his entire workplace he knows of only three people, including himself, who have been faithful to their spouses. I talked to a firefighter recently who said that adultery is expected in that community. In fact, he claims that firefighters themselves say you can trust a firefighter with your life, but not with your wife. (Obviously, there are exceptions—the firefighter who told me this is a godly deacon of the church where I serve.)

I wish I could say this were true only of people in secular workplaces. The horrible truth is that in recent years and months there has been a rash of high-profile pastors and religious leaders who have given in to the temptation to engage in adultery. Even among those who know the Bible better than anyone, there are those who have fallen for the devil's lie which says, "You can take God's good gift out of the context for which He created it and there will be no consequences. You can know fullness and freedom outside of His ordained framework."

The world is pushing to normalize homosexual behavior. The pressure has become so acute that many even in conservative evangelicalism have somehow reinterpreted the Bible to allow for this. For years, the church has treated same-sex attraction as a problem that is outside the bounds of polite conversation, outside the bounds of our ability to help, and implicitly outside the bounds of the gospel's power. Consequently, many in the church who struggle with same-sex attraction have been left with only one voice to listen to as it pertains to this temptation—the voice of the world, the flesh, and the devil, saying, "This is the way you've been made, and if you deny yourself fulfillment in this area, you will never be happy. Don't you want to be free?"

You can see the lie in our culture, observe it in our advertising and entertainment, and hear it in the tempting whispers of your own mind. "Have sex before marriage. Have sex outside of marriage. Have sex with someone of the same gender. Don't be shackled by God's unreasonable rules; He's just keeping something good from you. Don't you want to be free?" This is the voice of the serpent still speaking.

On the other hand, Jesus would tell you that sin is an enslaver. Whoever commits sin is the slave of sin. Just like God giving Adam that first command in the garden, His giving us this good gift of sexuality exclusively for enjoyment within monogamous, heterosexual marriage is not denying us something good; He's protecting us from something destructive.

Listen, you who are tempted to stray from your marriage. Listen, you who are struggling with same-sex attraction. You could live for 1,000 years, but you will never hear a true believer say, "I praise God I committed adultery; it has been so edifying to me and those around me." "I'm so glad I've given myself over to homosexual desires; now I truly enjoy the fullness of fellowship with Jesus Christ." You will never hear that because sin is universally destructive. God, who is love, would protect us from it and would offer us something so much better. In this book, we've spent much time looking at this ideal, marital love of the Song—two people enjoying one another in ways that the world could only dream about. That kind of love and sexual fulfillment can only be known inside of a covenant marriage.

If you're on the front end of temptation and haven't given in, but you're being bombarded by it, don't believe the devil; *believe Jesus*. That sin will not make you free; it will enslave you. Jesus makes you free. Run to Jesus. Do that by telling a fellow member of your church about your temptation. Ask him for help. Don't be afraid that he is going to think you're weird for having sexual temptation—he's had it, too. Keep in mind that when you're in a room full of human beings, you're in a room full of people who have failed sexually. Some have had relations before marriage, some have committed adultery, and some have entertained homosexual desires and acted on those desires. Don't let the notion that you're alone or unique prevent you from asking for help.

Hope After Breached Boundaries

Perhaps, right now you're demoralized, fearing that because of past failures you are hopelessly stained and cannot enjoy God's good gifts. Perhaps, you're thinking, "I've ruined it; and I'm ruined." There are consequences for sin, to be sure. However, let's not commit the further sin of living as if there is not a living Savior.

Consider the following words from 1 Corinthians 6:9–10: "Do not be deceived: neither the sexually immoral, nor idolaters, nor adulterers, nor men who practice homosexuality, nor thieves, nor the greedy, nor drunkards, nor revilers, nor swindlers will inherit the kingdom of God." Who among us cannot find ourselves somewhere in that text? We were all idolaters from birth. Many of us have been sexually immoral, adulterers, or practiced homosexuality. None of these kinds of people inherit the kingdom of God.

But, oh, what a word in verse 11: "And such were some of you. But you were washed, you were sanctified, you were justified in the name of the Lord Jesus Christ and by the Spirit of our God." The church of Jesus Christ is composed of people who *were* these things, but by the work of Jesus Christ are these things no more. You may have repented of these sins, sought forgiveness, been forgiven, and yet somehow have made that past failure part of your current identity. Don't you dare! You are not the sexually immoral. You are not an adulterer. You are not a homosexual. If you have repented and trusted in Christ, *He* is your identity!

Satan always lies. He lies before we give in: "This will be great— fullness and freedom, removed from the harsh constraints of a tyrant God." He also lies after we give in: "This is who you are now. You'll never be anything else. You're ruined. Just own it." When you are tempted to go back to that place of sin, to think of yourself as sexually immoral, to think of yourself as an adulterer, or to identify as a homosexual, answer the lies of the devil with the truth of 1 Corinthians 6:11: *That was me, but I was washed, I was sanctified, I was justified in the name of the Lord Jesus Christ and by the Spirit of my God.* The gospel is true.

Still, you may be thinking, "Yes, this is true about my identity, but has my past sin ruined my ability to enjoy God's good gifts in the future? Can I ever know the love of the Song?" In the prophecy of Joel, we see the character of God which answers that question.

The prophet Joel wrote to a nation of spiritual adulterers, whoring after every god on every high hill under every green tree. God purposed to bring judgment upon them in the form of invaders, depicted in Joel as a plague of locusts stripping the land bare of the implements of worship. No more grain, no more oil, no more wine. No more ability to approach the One True God in worship. In other words, the judgment for their spiritual adultery was the loss of the good gift of fellowship with God. Yet, during Joel's pronouncement of judgment, he offers hope:

'Yet even now,' declares the LORD, 'return to me with all your heart, with fasting, with weeping, and with mourning; and rend your hearts and not your garments.' Return to the LORD your God, for he is gracious and merciful, slow to anger, and abounding in steadfast love; and he relents over disaster. Who knows whether he will not turn and relent, and leave a blessing behind him, a grain offering and a drink offering for the LORD your God? (Joel 2:12–14).

Just a few verses later comes a promise of fulfillment:

Be glad, O children of Zion, and rejoice in the LORD your God, for he has given the early rain for your vindication; he has poured down for you abundant rain, the early and the latter rain, as before. The threshing floors shall be full of grain; the vats shall overflow with wine and oil. I will restore to you the years that the swarming locust has eaten, the hopper, the destroyer, and the cutter, my great army, which I sent among you. You shall eat in plenty and be satisfied, and praise the name of the LORD your God, who has dealt wondrously with you. And my people shall never again be put to shame (Joel 2:23–26).

It is part of the kind character of our God to allow us to feel the loss of forfeited good gifts. However, says Joel, it is also part of His character to give those gifts back upon repentance. Is not this what we experienced in the loss of Eden, but returned to us through repentance and faith in Christ? Now, I'm not asserting that Joel teaches that if you've sinned sexually God guarantees the return of sexual fullness to you, but he does present a God of whom it is characteristic to do such things.

The church of Jesus Christ is filled with people who would testify to you about God's great grace and generosity in this area. There are many people who would say, "I gave into temptation before marriage, I committed adultery, I entertained homosexual desire; but I repented and by God's grace and generosity, He gave back what I forfeited. I enjoy intimacy in my marriage far beyond anything I ever dreamed possible." There is going to be brokenness to overcome. There is going to be difficulty. You may not enjoy it as quickly as you would have had you not given into temptation, but here is the good news: we have a God whose character says, "I give back good gifts forfeited by sin. You repent; I give them back." You may have shackled yourself with sin. You may have cheated yourself from a gift. By grace He gives it back in fullness and freedom. The gospel is true. Glory to the Lord Jesus Christ.

Discussion Questions/Activities

1. In what ways do you feel the culture pushing you to question the wisdom of God's protective context for His good marital gifts?

2. How does the Song depict the blesssedness of remaining within God's boundaries for marriage? What are those blessings?

3. In what ways are you most tempted to breach those boundaries?

4. In what ways might a marriage experience temporal difficulties as a result of breaching God's boundaries in these ways?

5. If you have already breached those boundaries, what hope does 1 Corinthians 6:9–11 offer? What about Joel 2:12–14?

14

OUTRO

A Real-Life, Gospel-Commending Marriage

"I don't love you anymore," she said. "I'm only staying for the girls."

This book began with the story of a fictitious couple named Dan and Vanessa, an amalgamation of numerous couples I've counseled over the years. The above words come from a real marriage, a true story about what can happen when two people find themselves in a fractured relationship but decide to pursue faithfulness to Christ above all things.

Aaron and Christi had great expectations coming into marriage, but as so many find, it was no fairy tale.[1] They married young and became pregnant unexpectedly the first year. Aaron was finishing nursing school and trying desperately to provide so that Christi could be a stay-at-home mother. In just a few short years, their quiver had expanded to four daughters. The reality of adult responsibilities and financial stress, compounded with a host of unmet expectations and mutual self-seeking, led to a trend of hurtful words spoken on both

---

[1] I had a front row seat to this story, as Aaron and Christi are my brother-in-law and sister. They were happy to allow me to share it, for which I am grateful.

sides. An inability to biblically communicate provided fertile soil for seeds of bitterness to spread like ground cover in their hearts. Both tried in their own way to prod the other to change, but eventually, they both realized there was no use. "This is just the way it's going to be." And just like that, in the span of five short years, all hope for a fulfilling marriage gave way to something that felt more like a business relationship.

This is where so many marriages go and where husbands and wives are tempted to stay. This temptation hit Aaron and Christi hard, but in accordance with the Scriptures, the Lord was faithful in their temptation to provide a way of escape.[2] Through a series of gracious events—and their godly responses—He transformed the marriage.

First, Christi was converted after thinking most of her life that she was already saved. An inductive study of Hebrews led her to realize she had never surrendered her life to the Lord, had never borne the fruit of repentance, had never known Christ. She repented, trusted Him, and began to radically change as she submitted to the Word.

Second, someone on the outside of the marriage loved Aaron enough to confront his self-centeredness, and Aaron had the wisdom to listen. A heart change took place in him that can only be characterized as repentance, and he began to make a lifestyle out of Christlike service to everyone around him, especially Christi.

Third, they agreed to go to counseling. While Christi had been converted and was growing and Aaron had begun to serve her, much still needed to change. Their inability to communicate was a serious issue and a major reason that they still felt like mere roommates. A family member offered to pay for counseling, if they would go. They did. The communication skills alone were a great help and set the marriage on an upward trajectory.

Fourth, Aaron and Christi joined a gospel-driven church. Hearing the good news of Jesus Christ week after week, being called to live in light of it, learning the biblical roles of a husband and wife, and striving for personal holiness led them to the place where their marriage now bears no resemblance to the broken union of those early years. Aaron

---

[2] 1 Cor. 10:13: "No temptation has overtaken you that is not common to man. God is faithful, and he will not let you be tempted beyond your ability, but with the temptation he will also provide the way of escape, that you may be able to endure it."

loves his wife as Jesus loves the church. He pours himself out for Christi and their daughters. Likewise, Christi is the picture of loving submission, responding to Aaron as the church does to Jesus. Though they were close to settling for a passionless, self-seeking marriage, by God's grace they found something better. As they have grown to love Jesus more deeply, they have come to love one another well. Those close to them can testify they adore each other.

Recently, my wife and I were having ice cream with Aaron and Christi. We began to discuss the concept of remarrying after being widowed. Christi said nonchalantly, "I could never remarry. I've already had the perfect husband." I silently praised God. He alone could bring these two from "I don't love you anymore" to "I've already had the perfect husband."

What To Do Now

The Song of Songs is about divine, marital love exemplified by Christ and emulated by believers. This love can be yours. If the gospel is true, and we are believers, this love is God's design, and He generously gives to all who wholeheartedly follow Him. We need only to wholeheartedly pursue it.

What might be some wise next steps? **First, reread this book.** Humans are forgetful creatures, particularly as it pertains to the things of the Lord. This is why we find Him saying the same things over and over in the Scriptures. If we leave any helpful book, sermon, or teaching behind and move on to something else...we leave it behind and move on to something else. It takes intentionality to apply these things. Perhaps in a second reading, you could prayerfully look for the top three areas addressed by the Song on which the Lord would have you concentrate. If you already know what those areas are, devise a plan to put these things into practice. Knowledge unapplied only puffs up, and conviction that does not lead to follow-through will only sear the conscience.[3]

---

[3] 1 Cor. 8:1–2: "This 'knowledge' puffs up, but love builds up. If anyone imagines that he knows something, he does not yet know as he ought to know." 1 Tim 1:18–19: "This charge I entrust to you, Timothy, my child, in accordance with the prophecies previously made about you, that by them you may wage the good warfare, holding faith and a good conscience. By rejecting this, some have made shipwreck of their faith."

Second, read the Song devotionally. This book that once appeared to us as uncomfortably erotic Hebrew poetry should now be one of the richest sources of devotional material in the whole Bible. As you read the text, think of the love of Christ in personal terms. "This is *my* beloved and this is *my* friend" (5:16). Let the Song's pictures of the gospel take you to the cross, empty tomb, and eternal throne, from which even now Jesus intercedes for you, His beloved. Gazing at this wonderful Savior should motivate us to be like Him. As you read the Song, pray for wisdom and help to follow in the footsteps of Christ and to love your spouse as He has loved you.

Third, consider counseling. No book can provide everything any given couple needs. While I have tried to give some helpful practical suggestions, this book was intended mainly to expose readers to the love of Christ in the Song and give a vision for the kind of love that is possible for those who believe. If you recognize yourself as someone settling for a legally-intact, but loveless marriage, it's likely the case that you need more help than this book can give. If you are in that situation, I have three pieces of counsel for you. First, don't despair—books aren't counselors. People are counselors. You need good biblical counseling, and there is plenty of it out there if you'll take the time to find it. Second, if this book is moving you to take that step and get the help you need from a counselor, praise the Lord that He used this book in your life as it was intended. Third, don't wait to get that help. Time is only going to temper your resolve to change. Strike while the iron is hot. Decide today, based on the character of Christ and His trustworthiness, that you'll commit to following Him in loving this way.

If you need counseling, I would suggest talking to your pastor. Sadly, some pastors do not counsel. In that case, I highly recommend The Association of Certified Biblical Counselors (biblicalcounseling.com). You can search this website for a counselor in your area.

Fourth, strive to believe the gospel. I know that many, if not most, reading this book are already converted Christians. However, there is a sense in which the hardest part of living the Christian life is believing that the gospel is true in every day circumstances. When we become gospel-deficient in our spiritual diet, it is all too easy to live as if Jesus can only die for sins, but He can't change hearts. For that reason, return daily to the Scriptures and be reminded of a complete Savior. He is in the business of binding up what is broken and working in others the love He exemplifies.

> "Now to him who is able to do far more abundantly than all
> that we ask or think,
> according to the power at work within us,
> to him be glory in the church and in Christ Jesus
> throughout all generations, forever and ever. Amen."
> (Eph. 3:20–21)

Bibliography

Brauns, Chris. *Unpacking Forgiveness: Biblical Answers For Complex Questions And Deep Wounds*. Wheaton, IL: Crossway, 2008.

Calvin, John. *Institutes of the Christian Religion*, n.d.

Downey, Dave. "Firestorm 2003: The Story of a Catastrophe." *The San Diego Union-Tribune*, November 16, 2003. https://www.sandiegouniontribune.com/sdut-firestorm-2003-the-story-of-a-catastrophe-2003nov16-story.html.

Duguid, Iain M. *Song of Songs*. Reformed Expository Commentary. Phillipsburg, New Jersey: P&R Publishing, 2016.

Garrett, Duane A., and Dr. Paul R House. *Song of Songs and Lamentations*. Vol. 23B. Word Biblical Commentary. Grand Rapids: Zondervan, 2018.

Mohammed, Ravelle. "Pat Robertson Blasted for Alzheimer's Divorce Advice." *The Christian Post*, September 14, 2011, sec. Church & Ministries. https://www.christianpost.com/news/pat-robertson-blasted-for-alzheimers-divorce-advice.html.

O'Donnell, Douglas Sean. *The Song of Solomon: An Invitation to Intimacy*. Preaching the Word. Wheaton, Illinois: Crossway, 2012.

Perry, Tony. "35-Year-Old Sentenced in Deadly Cedar Fire." *Los Angeles Times*, November 18, 2005. https://www.latimes.com/archives/la-xpm-2005-nov-18-me-cedar18-story.html.

Piper, John. "Getting to the Bottom of Your Joy." *Desiring God* (blog), January 3, 2001. https://www.desiringgod.org/messages/getting-to-the-bottom-of-your-joy.

Ryle, J. C. *Holiness: Its Nature, Hindrances, Difficulties, and Roots*. Carlisle, PA: Banner of Truth Trust, 2014.

———. *Thoughts For Young Men: Updated Edition With Study Guide*. Vol. 1. Christian Manliness Series. Cedar Lake, MI: Waymark, 2018.

Scott, Stuart. *The Exemplary Husband: A Biblical Perspective*. Bemidji, MN: Focus Pub., 2002.

Stetzer, Ed. "On Marriage and Alzheimer's Disease: Listen to Robertson McQuilkin and Not Pat Robertson." *Christianity Today*, September 15, 2011, sec. Culture, Leadership.

https://www.christianitytoday.com/edstetzer/2011/september/on-marriage-and-alzheimers-disease-listen-to-robertson.html.

Zylstra, Sarah Eekhoff. "Died: Robertson McQuilkin, College President Praised for Alzheimer's Resignation." *Christianity Today*, June 2, 2016. https://www.christianitytoday.com/news/2016/june/died-robertson-mcquilkin-columbia-president-alzheimers-ciu.html.

Made in the USA
Columbia, SC
07 April 2022

58627730R00124